THE LEGACY OF LIGHT

The Legacy of Light:
A history of Irish windows

Nessa Roche

with photography by
Hugh MacConville

Wordwell

First published in 1999
Wordwell Ltd
PO Box 69, Bray, Co. Wicklow
Copyright © Wordwell 1999.

Cover design: Nick Maxwell and Rachel Dunne.

ISBN 1 869857 31 3

British Library Cataloguing-in-Publication Data.
A catalogue record for this book is available from the British Library.

This publication has received support from the Heritage Council under the 1999 Publications Grant Scheme.

Typeset in Ireland by Wordwell Ltd.

Book design: Nick Maxwell.

Origination by Wordwell Ltd.

Printed by Brookfield Printing Company.

All photographs © Hugh MacConville except where indicated.

CONTENTS

ACKNOWLEDGEMENTS

The idea for a book on Irish windows grew out of research carried out for a doctoral thesis on the development of the window in Irish architecture. A very large number of people around the country gave freely of their time and knowledge, while others gave the author free rein to inspect their homes. They are acknowledged elsewhere, but I would like to remember their kindness and to thank them again.

The Legacy of Light stemmed from a conversation between Hugh MacConville and me at the launch of *Ireland's Earthen Houses*, which Hugh produced with Frank MacDonald and Peigín Doyle in 1997. Our initial thoughts were given a great deal of impetus by a publication grant awarded by the Heritage Council. Financial assistance was generously given also by *Dúchas*, the Irish Georgian Society, Niall O'Donoghue of Donevin Estates and W. & J. Bolger Ltd.

Not all of the photographs we took could be included, but we are very grateful to all of the householders who quizzically tolerated our photographing their windows. We know only some of their names, such as Michael and Annette Hogan in Bonnettstown; Jo O'Leary in Kanturk; Brigitta Lennon, Swiftsheath; Mrs Foley, Lismore; the O'Braonains in Castlecomer; Desmond Guinness; and the owners of the delightful Cigar Divan in Carlow.

Many thanks to Peter Pearson for writing a preface for us, and for sharing his knowledge over the years. David Griffin kindly led us in the direction of period illustrations and let his office become a meeting room for Hugh and me. Maurice Craig gave us permission to quote a lovely passage from *Dublin 1660–1860* (Penguin, 1952).

Permission to reproduce period drawings and prints was kindly supplied by Mary Clark, archivist of Dublin Corporation; the OPW/*Dúchas* photography department; the Drapers' Company, London; the Board of the Architectural Archive; Lord Belmore; Peter Francis; and the Trustees of the National Library of Ireland. *Dúchas* kindly supplied the photograph of Carrick-on-Suir Castle, while Michael O'Connell gave us the photo of Rock Cottage, Co. Antrim, and several more photographs were taken by Ian Lumley. The diagrams were drawn by the author.

The staff at Wordwell effortlessly carried out the job of transforming raw text and individual photographs into a finished book; particular thanks are due to Nick Maxwell and Emer Condit. Peigín Doyle transformed the original academic text into something more readily accessible and made other contributions as the book took shape. Thanks are also due to Primary Colour for technical assistance and to Cormac MacConville for physical help on the long photographic expeditions.

Lastly, the families and friends who allowed us to spread our light box, slides and draft typescripts on kitchen and office tables deserve our warm thanks.

PREFACE

The publication of this book coincides with an emerging public awareness of Ireland's architectural history. People are coming to appreciate the many fine qualities of old buildings and their details, and now consider, for example, keeping the old render on a house, the original slates from the roof or the finely made windows and doors. There is the beginning of an understanding that the keeping of an old building is as much an art as a science.

Living with old uneven floorboards and ancient plaster is part of the charm of being in a historic building. If it is all replaced and made new, even and shiny, then the sense of age and the feeling of history have gone.

Nowhere is this more obvious than in the windows, part of the public façade which addresses the street and says much about the character and beauty of the building.

This book, which is the culmination of many years of research and practical work by Nessa Roche and is illustrated by the photographs of Hugh MacConville, presents a whole new perspective on the history of Irish buildings. The result is a publication which underlines the importance of the authentic window in each and every type of old building in the country.

Sadly, a massive amount of destruction—the tearing out of original windows—has taken place and is still taking place all over Ireland. No part of the country, no village, no town or city has escaped the ugly mockery of uPVC window replacement. Many well-meaning property-owners are persuaded that their windows are beyond repair and must be replaced. It is interesting that many auctioneers now recognise that replacement windows (aluminium, uPVC or even crude wooden copies) actually devalue historic properties and old houses.

This book explains how the traditional window evolved and why it was made in a certain way. Chapters are devoted to the classical tradition, the special Irish window types, and the Georgian and Victorian styles. All aspects of window joinery are examined and the conservation issues explained. There is also much about the history of glass-making in Ireland, showing the fascinating methods which were used to produce the beautiful old glass which, unfortunately, people are still throwing away on a daily basis when they discard their seemingly 'rotten' old windows.

This timely book is a beautifully illustrated history of an unusual subject, but it is also designed to campaign for the protection and retention of what is left of our 'legacy of light'—our old windows.

Peter Pearson
November 1999

Cape Clear, Co. Cork.

INTRODUCTION: WINDOWS—LIFE AND LIGHT

Many people do not realise that our architecture is just as distinctively Irish as our music or landscape. The buildings of Ireland, like bare mountains and rolling farmland, are part of what identifies this country. For centuries a particular philosophy of architectural design, called classicism, held sway in Ireland. Proportion and light governed the design of buildings, and therefore the size and position of the windows were of immense importance. The arrangement of the windows (termed the fenestration) has formed the character of Irish buildings for many centuries. From the smallest cottage to the grandest Georgian mansion, the windows of almost all buildings were arranged according to these classical principles. The resulting design and shapes genuinely attract us.

In the eighteenth and nineteenth centuries a marvellous agreement of style was reached in the design of Irish buildings. Most were not architectural set pieces; they were not laid out with the precision of the best architects of the day. The majority were put up by masons and carpenters, with a hand from pattern books and perhaps the input of a dabbling amateur. Overall, they created a pleasantly unpretentious style of streetscape, enlivened by the window design alone, including shop fronts. This is what makes a tour through any Irish town or city so interesting to those whose eyes have been opened to the beauty of our windows.

In Ireland we are much preoccupied with light and weather. Our northern latitude gives us a wonderful blue-grey tone of light which has long been celebrated in landscape painting. Windows, linking the outside world and the familiar rooms of home, reflect that light, as cloud formations seem to dance on the irregular surface of old glass, and intermittent shafts of sunlight flash off the panes. The light of a summer's evening shows Ireland off to its best advantage. The angled, soft-hued light brings alive the old glass in windows, which sparkles with a fiery glow as the sun sets, enlivening the whole building.

Maurice Craig, the noted architectural historian, spoke fondly of the windows of the Old Library at Trinity College, Dublin: 'Only when, on a winter's day, seen from the top of a tram in Dawson Street across the Fellows' Garden, every pane of the old crown glass suddenly flashes with orange fire, only at such moments does this huge building seem to relax its customary

As the importance of classical proportions and regularity declined, different types and arrangements of windows started to appear. New styles of window shapes became popular, and the use of arched windows became widespread. The late nineteenth-century boardroom of the Listowel Arms Hotel is lit by a triple window (details in threes were always popular), which, each sash glazed with a single pane, was fully modern in outlook. Owing to its position in a corner of the main square this unusual window is probably overlooked by most visitors.

expression of measured reticence'.

Ever since the first shelters were erected, people have sought to have as much light as possible inside their homes, but only in this century have developments in building construction and glass-making progressed to such a degree that windows can be made to any conceivable size and the masonry walls dispensed with. This is rightly seen as one of the most important changes ever to have taken place in architecture. However, as windows grew to encompass the whole of the building, they lost the individuality and character that came from the relationship of their size to the other elements of the façade.

Windows in everyday buildings suffered the same treatment. As architects began experimenting with huge windows, the classical tradition faded from view. The rules of proportion which had so long governed fenestration were dispensed with and almost forgotten. With only a few exceptions the results are disappointing.

We need to reclaim these rules of proportion and apply them to new materials, not in a slavish way but returning to the principle that a building can be a thing of beauty with windows of appropriate size, scale and position.

Alone among architectural features the window faces both inward and outward, a part both of the public life of our towns or countryside and of the unseen private space of each inhabitant. As much as we need light inside, we all need to look out. But in looking past our windows we ignore the contribution they are constantly making to our homes, both inside and outside. The character of individual buildings and of our streets and roadsides is formed by the nature of the windows. The addition of an interestingly shaped window gives a focal point to a building. Buildings with very few windows are forbidding, while those with a profusion of windows are perceived to be far more welcoming.

In Ireland we have only lately been awakened to the attractions of our built heritage. This is clearly seen in our callous disposal of the features of our old buildings—notably windows—and their replacement by ones of ill-suited design and materials.

I hope that everyone who reads this book will look afresh at the mundane and familiar window, and appreciate where it came from and how it makes Ireland unique in architectural terms.

Much of the original glass survives in the West Front of Trinity College, Dublin. For almost 250 years it has shimmered when lit up by the evening sun, catching and distorting the busy life of College Green and the old Parliament House. The combination of old glass and softened stone (here unfortunately polluted) is irreplaceable; luckily Trinity College is aware of its value. Most of the university buildings retain their wonderful eighteenth- and nineteenth-century windows and glass, a marvellous testament to the benefits of maintenance.

Listowel, Co. Kerry.

1. WHY OUR BUILDINGS LOOK THE WAY THEY DO —PROPORTIONS IN IRISH WINDOW DESIGN

In the fourteenth and fifteenth centuries, Italian architects, philosophers and mathematicians, dissatisfied with the narrow outlook of the Gothic age, turned to the surviving ruins and writings of the Romans for inspiration. This search for truth in art and philosophy through the study of ancient civilisations became known as the Renaissance, or rebirth.

It quickly became clear that geometry and proportion had been used in the design of Greek and Roman buildings. A number of standard decorative features, such as columns, pediments, cornices, porticos and arcades, had been employed.

The use of geometry was so convenient and the buildings produced by it were held to be so beautiful by Renaissance thinkers that classical proportion in buildings was seen as the expression of universal laws of beauty laid down by God.

Palladian principles

The Italian architect Andrea Palladio was one of the foremost Renaissance architects who wrote about the ancient laws of architectural harmony. Palladio (and contemporary writers Alberti and Serlio) held that, externally, beauty in building flowed from the relationship of all the parts of a building to each other and to the whole: 'that the structure may appear an entire and compleat body, wherein each member agrees with the other'.

In 1570 Palladio published his *Four Books of Architecture*, in which he dissected the geometry of ancient Roman buildings. His ideal proportions for windows, rooms and whole façades were based upon the square, cube or Golden Section (see pp 14–15), arranged in a careful, measured manner.

Along with this Renaissance reverence for proportion was a universal respect for light, because without light man cannot survive. To the learned and inquiring minds of this time, the architecture of the preceding Gothic age, with its dark, low domestic interiors, symbolised a closed, suspicious mentality. In contrast, the Renaissance was open to humanist learning and to light. According to philosophers, light would spring-clean the psyche and introduce rationality to a modern world.

Leamaneh Castle in County Clare was built in two stages: the earlier tower-house with tiny defensive loop windows is nearest the camera. It was added to in the latest Irish Renaissance fashion in the early seventeenth century, with large and impressive mullioned and transomed windows. These stone supports were necessary because glazed lights could not safely be made in large sizes. Even so, these windows represented a major step forward in terms of indoor comfort—and displayed the taste and security of the O'Brien family, confident of their status.

Bonnettstown, Co. Kilkenny, exemplifies all that is graceful about Irish classical houses. Built in the 1730s, when Palladian ideals were taking root, it has a façade decorated only by stone architraves on the windows and door, giving due prominence to the main floor. Without pediments or porticos, houses like Bonnettstown relied on fenestration for their effect. Two minor details show this house to be provincial—the tall upper-floor windows (normally shorter than on the main floor) and six windows per floor, where an odd number is usual and makes it easier to design a central door. The sashes are late eighteenth-century, but some original oak sashes survive in one side wall.

One of the most visible effects of classical architecture, wrote Raymond McGrath (at one time chief architect of the Office of Public Works), was that windows were marshalled and disciplined as never before. By the time Mountjoy Square was built (from 1792) few designers thought of deviating from the classical school, so ingrained had it become. One slight difference between this and earlier terraces is the placing of the first-floor window-sills near to floor level, to encourage the feeling of openness and nearness to the outside. Hence so many houses have little wrought- and cast-iron balconets, placed more for decoration than for protection for unwary lovers of the bracing Dublin air.

Provincial house-builders, however far from Dublin fashions, still paid attention to classical fenestration. In this house in Fethard, Co. Tipperary, the top-floor windows are not as small as they should be; perhaps they were altered late in the last century, when the glazing bars were removed from all the sashes and single panes of glass were fitted to let in more light. The building looks bare—a common complaint in many Irish towns, which are often criticised for their greyness. However, look closely and see that in order to compensate for the loss of texture each window was dressed with a stucco surround in a vernacular/classical style.

The Wide Streets Commissioners laid down very exacting rules about façade design in Dublin. This 1784 plan for part of Dame Street shows the gradual reduction in window size towards the attic floor, and the spacing is arranged so that all the windows in the terrace are equidistant. There is no other ornament, but the shop fronts seem very grand to our eyes and the arched windows give the impression of a continuous arcade. By shading in the glazing of the shop windows the artist is copying the impression of light and shade imparted by crown glass.

Several practical factors restrained this Renaissance desire for light in buildings. The most important was the need to build strongly and securely. Therefore the lowest or basement floor was often given few, small windows, to give the whole edifice the appearance of having a solid foundation. There was a real concern for safe construction. It was feared that windows placed near the corners would imperil the whole structure at the vital corner joints and that windows placed too close to each other would weaken the walls.

To help support the walls, Renaissance architects favoured placing all windows directly above those on the ground floor, and making them taller than they were wide because there is less pressure on a short lintel or window head. This, allied with the desire for light, gave rise to the belief that good architecture involved the proper positioning of windows.

These theories of proportion in architectural design gradually spread to other countries, carried by foreign nobles and travellers anxious to show off their familiarity with fashion. Many books were published on classical design, some of which made their way to Ireland.

Stretching the rules

In Italian Renaissance designs, window openings were relatively small and widely spaced, as shade, rather than light, was important in the hot, bright Mediterranean climate. Later, architects in northern Europe stretched these rules because buildings in colder, duller regions had a greater need for daylight. By then—the early seventeenth century—classicism had become the prevailing architectural style throughout much of Europe.

In the early eighteenth century, architects again began to use Palladio's system of proportions in the design of rooms and façades. This new approach became known as Neo-Palladianism. In Ireland, Neo-Palladianism is commonly called Georgian after the kings during whose reigns it was popular. The design of the whole façade was based on the main parts of a classical column. In other words, the house base was the column pedestal, the main floors formed the shaft, and the area above the cornice represented the capital. This meant that the main floors had to be substantially taller than the base, and the parapet/roof had to be very small in proportion.

For the Neo-Palladians, the ideal proportions for building were all extensions of the cube. While detached houses could have long, impressive façades, it became usual to have tall, narrow terraced houses in towns, with dimensions of one and a half to two and a half squares—that is, up to two and

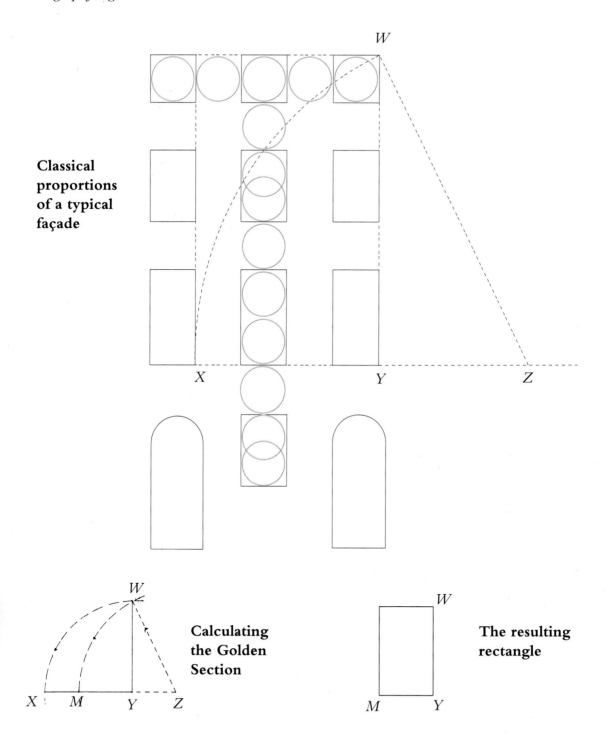

**Classical
proportions
of a typical
façade**

**Calculating
the Golden
Section**

**The resulting
rectangle**

Geometric diagram of window and classical façade proportions.

Ideally, every façade in a classical building had its windows proportioned by a precise mathematical code, worked out using basic modules such as circles and rectangles with the help of geometry. Filling in the façade with circles, as is done here, is a convenient way to illustrate how the same module was used to determine the proportions of each window. Here the module is three feet six inches, a common window width. The windows themselves were usually based on percentages of a square and were normally between one and two squares tall. The dotted lines show how the upper-floor windows are contained within a large rectangle, which here is calculated using the Golden Section.

The Golden Section is a geometric principle of the ancient classical builders which was avidly taken up during the Renaissance. It is the division of a line by an exactly calculated proportion requiring the use of mathematical instruments. It was held to be an especially significant proportion, from which rectangles and cubic measurements could be designed for a satisfactory visual result. A single window can be designed using a rectangle based on this principle, or alternatively the glazing bars may be calculated by using it in a rectangle about one and a half times as high as it is wide.

Calculation: The object is to find the Golden Section of line x–y. This is done by extending the line x–y by half its original distance to a point z. At y draw a vertical line of the same height as the original line x–y and call the end-point of this line w. Then draw an arc from z, using w as the radius. Where it cuts the line x–z is the Golden Section, point m. A rectangle can be drawn using m, y and w to give a rectangle based on the Golden Section.

Order in fenestration became universal in Ireland as the eighteenth century progressed—the general rule was that one placed the windows over each other and equidistant from those on the same floor. Even in the furthest removed settlement, such as Cape Clear, the message was plain—pay attention to the fenestration and the building will fit in. Simple, upright houses like these are distinctively Irish; their details vary but their proportions rarely differ much from the basic classical model.

a half times as high as they were wide. In Irish Georgian houses, especially in the later eighteenth century, the roof was often hidden to better achieve this proportion.

A vertical emphasis in the façade was seen as essential to balance the horizontal lines of design elements such as the plinth, string-courses and cornice. Regular rows of tall windows were used in Palladian classicism to give this vertical emphasis, so that the form of the window became an essential part of the design of the whole building.

In Ireland the exteriors of buildings were rarely ornamented with the columns, porticos and plaster relief so beloved of Renaissance architects. Almost all decoration was reserved for the inside, and Irish designers relied on the ordering of the windows alone, enlivened by a decorative doorway, for surface interest. This gave Irish Georgian architecture a style which was unique to this country.

Positioning windows

As windows became more important in the overall design, positioning them correctly became a critical consideration. They had to be sited harmoniously within the whole width of the building, avoiding the corners and set suitably far apart. The width of the façade was divided up to see how many windows would sit comfortably in it. The space between each window was preferably as wide as, or slightly wider than, the window itself so as not to give too crowded an impression. Windows on the same floor are always the same size unless one is arched.

Placement of the windows did not depend on external measurements alone. Inside, they had to be placed at a convenient height so that one could look out while sitting down, and they had to stop below the decorated cornice of the room. On the exterior this usually left a space of about four feet between the lintels and the sills of the windows above.

Harmony by module

Many Georgian buildings and squares were built by speculative developers. These builders were not trained classicists but they found an ingenious way to bring classical principles into the design of their buildings. They broke down the classical proportions into modular measurements in which there were just a few standard sizes. The width of the windows was the most important modular measurement. There were several common widths, such as 4ft to 4ft 6ins in larger houses and between 3ft and 3ft 6ins in more modest dwellings and out-offices. One tends to think of modular buildings with standardised components as a modern innovation, but these eighteenth-century builders were masters of the art and achieved the ideal proportions by this simple rule of thumb.

By using these standard measurements, the simplest mason and village craftsman were able to incorporate ancient principles of proportion and harmony into the humblest building. The measurements and ratios could be learned by on-the-job training or from pattern books. In this way, the traditional Irish cottage and the modest town house came to share with the grandest Georgian mansion the harmonious proportions of ancient Greek and Roman architecture. Out of this developed a harmony of style and proportion between different buildings and individual streets which gave an overall sense of unity and grace to Irish townscapes.

The traditional shop front is disappearing as fast as the local shop. Luckily some remain in the hands of appreciative owners, and can still be admired. Ó Bráonáin's shop in Castlecomer is, as its fascia sign says, a unique gift—an irreplaceable addition to the town. The shop front is in a carefully proportioned Ionic order, with fluted columns. The shop sits correctly in the centre of the whole façade, and its four sash windows are models of the kind with added stucco detailing that was once found countrywide. The house door and the window above it are set a little apart from the other windows, to visually and physically separate shop and residence.

Strandhill, Co. Sligo.

2. THE LONG JOURNEY TOWARDS LIGHT—FROM RENAISSANCE CASTLE TO GEORGIAN SQUARE

Irish history can be tracked through the style and shape of windows, which were determined by the political and economic conditions of the day. In medieval times, castles were built for defence rather than comfort and style. Until well into the seventeenth century, windows were only built where necessary and were placed haphazardly. They were very small and usually shaped like narrow slits to allow arrows or pistols to be fired from them. An occasional large window or two decorated the top floors, to light the great hall and the apartments of the lord and his family. These windows often had carved decoration, usually in the simple form of hood-moulds, but some sumptuous window surrounds are found in Galway, where Celtic motifs are carved into the stones dressing the windows.

The windows in all types of buildings were small and glass was rare, used only in Dublin Castle, for example, or the richer cathedrals. Oiled skin or paper and timber shutters kept out wind and rain. If glass was used, it was in small diamond panes, soldered together with lengths of lead.

The castles were very basic and dark, and probably cold much of the time. Life was lived outdoors, and all available money was put into food and defence. Comforts like glass windows had no place in this harsh world. Even after Renaissance principles of proportion in design became known in Ireland, life was too tough for native and settler alike to allow many to follow the classical ideals.

A window on wealth

Although it was rare to erect fashionable buildings, with regular large windows and expensive glass, some rich nobles did show off their wealth and modernity in this way. In the 1560s the earl of Ormond demonstrated his love for Queen Elizabeth and his confidence in his own local power in the design of his new castle in Carrick-on-Suir, Co. Tipperary. This building was well endowed with glazed windows—the glass was bought in Antwerp.

© DÚCHAS, THE HERITAGE SERVICE

The earl of Ormond demonstrated both his local power and his knowledge of the latest building arts at Carrick-on-Suir Castle, built in the 1560s. Such generous fenestration was previously unknown in Ireland, with eleven windows in the Great Hall alone. All were glazed with glass from Antwerp, and some were probably decorated with arms and other devices in stained glass. The hood-moulds or drip-labels over the windows were designed to throw off water; they were a standard 'Tudor' feature until the mid-seventeenth century.

Some decades later, McDonough McCarthy almost succeeded in erecting a palatial mansion at Kanturk, Co. Cork, with large mullioned and transomed windows arranged in the classical manner. But its size and obvious defensive strength proved threatening to his enemies, who betrayed him and stopped its construction. The building remains unfinished, and is now a national monument and a great example of the Irish Renaissance castle. The O'Briens of Leamaneh, Co. Clare, were more successful, occupying their castle until the 1740s (see p. 8), when they built anew in the Palladian style.

These well-windowed, massive structures reveal a change in attitude on the part of those living at the higher end of the social scale, from the defensive, inward-looking mentality of the medieval age to a powerful, outward-looking authority. Despite the political and military turmoil, the builders of such powerful edifices were looking ahead to a time of peace, civilisation, wealth and patronage of the arts.

Standards of living started to rise despite regular plundering and warfare. Opulence and the notion of taste were being imported from Europe, and large transparent windows were required for the comfortable indoor life that was aspired to. Despite continued conflict, Cromwellian chaos and the hazardous nature of life, castles evolved into defensive houses which eventually became country houses on farmed estates. These changes were being driven by fashion and taste, despite the realities of looting, burning and transplantation.

Planters' homes

Not everyone's home was a castle. Many of the planted counties were populated with tradesmen, grantees and farmers who built smaller houses, most of which have long since disappeared. These ranged from defensive enclosed farmhouses and yards to timber-framed cagework houses. Some contemporary maps show single-storey terraced houses laid out neatly with large cross-mullioned windows and a dormer or two (see pp 28–9) ↑ ordinary houses were a combination of rural Scottish and English styles transplanted to an unsettled Ireland.

Rural cabins

The cottages and cabins which housed the majority of the rural population

GRANGE Caſtle, near Clondalken, 6.ᴹ from *Dublin*

G:B: *del:* 1773.

By the time Gabriel Beranger drew Grange Castle in 1773 most people of any means had abandoned their tower-houses in favour of comfortable dwellings with sash windows. Others built on to the tower-house, presenting a more classical front in keeping with their status as gentleman farmers. The new house here is modest, but has a small Gothic patterned fanlight, its only external decoration. The larger windows contrast with the irregular small slits of the tower, which has had a few larger openings punched through for light.

were made of rubble, stone or clay. Some were temporary shacks of sods on the side of a field against a ditch. These small dwellings were built without thought of comfort. Windows were rare, and glass was unheard of. The ideals of light and proportion were out of reach, as unobtainable as wealth itself.

Urban houses

Some towns contained strong, defensive, castle-like houses which owed something to both classical and medieval tradition. A number survive in Kilkenny, Dalkey and Galway, showing the sort of building considered by the Irish to be a noble dwelling. But the relatively small windows of houses such as Lynch's Castle in Galway were scoffed at by foreign visitors more appreciative of grandeur than of solidity. Luke Gernon, who visited Ireland in 1620, wrote of Cork city that 'the building is of stone and built after the Irish forme, which is castlewise and with narrow windows more for strength than for beauty, but they begin to beautify it in better forme'.

John Dunton, an English bookseller who visited Galway in the late 1690s, was more scathing. He compared the buildings to prisons because of the dark interiors and the small, stone-mullioned windows. Such comments were regularly repeated by horrified foreigners during the eighteenth century.

Glazed windows

Those houses with glazed windows used small diamond-shaped panes set in lead. This is called quarry glazing, and the technique is similar to that used for stained glass. The glass panel was held in a wrought-iron frame or set directly into the wall. Hinged (casement) openings were more expensive, and many buildings probably did without. Casements were vulnerable to all sorts of hazards, especially storm damage. In Ireland they opened outwards and could not be safely fastened against wind.

The unwieldiness and weight of the leaded window meant that the sizes both of the whole window and of the panes of glass within it were limited. When large windows were used, they had to have uprights and cross-bars of timber or stone called mullions and transoms, and a secondary grid of wrought-iron bars to support the small panes.

Despite this, glass of any sort was a great improvement and led to the

The earl of Cork's almshouses in Youghal present a venerable appearance today, but were designed in 1613 with up-to-date fenestration, the windows large enough to provide well-lit interiors for the humble inhabitants—an almost revolutionary consideration for the time! While the wealthy merchants of towns like Youghal, Kilkenny or Drogheda could afford strong stone houses and glazed windows, most ordinary people did without, especially small farmers and unskilled labourers.

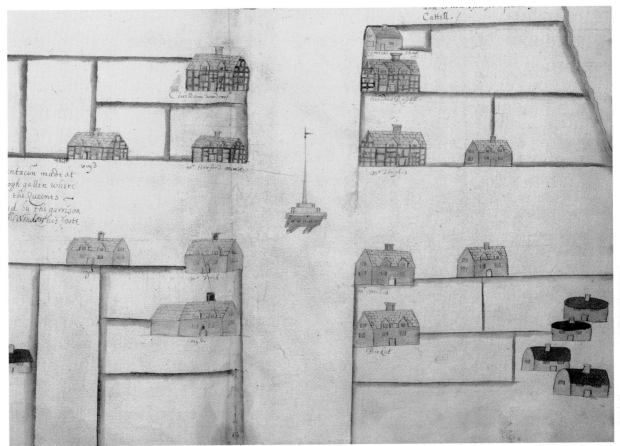

All over Ireland in the sixteenth and seventeenth centuries new settlers built villages like Moneymore, Co. Derry. They resembled English villages and owed nothing to classical proportioning. The windows were small, positioned wherever useful (and not consciously for effect). They were glazed with diamond or square panes in a framework of lead, similar to the technique used for stained glass. Some had outward-opening casements which caused their occupiers endless trouble owing to the windy Irish weather, with repairs a regular necessity.

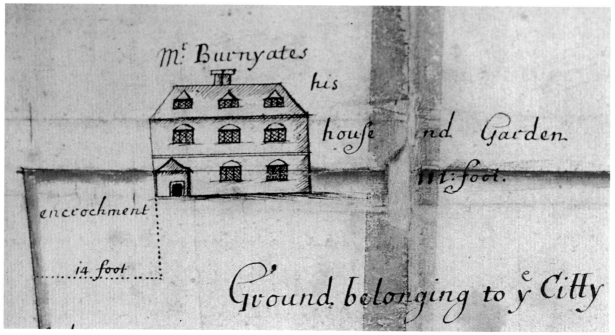

This illustration of Mr Burnyates's house and garden is one of the very few to show the type of house of an ordinary, albeit relatively prosperous, Dubliner in the seventeenth century. Drawn on a map of 1680, it shows large windows with several mullions (probably of timber), fitted with diamond-paned leaded lights. Note the dormer windows, which were very popular until the middle of the eighteenth century. The windows in houses like this provided basic lighting, as the diamond panes were small and the glass not very transparent. Although the windows all line up as in classical fenestration, the door is offset. Such small design failings continued to be common in urban terraces until the end of the nineteenth century.

development of the trades of glass-making and glazing. The demand for glazed windows was soon met through the establishment of glasshouses, in Ireland as well as in England. Joinery and the other arts involved in making windows, such as curtain-making, began to become common, especially later in the seventeenth century.

Restoration and peace

After the Restoration of King Charles II in 1660, life settled down into a peaceful pattern, and building started around the country. Dublin expanded at a tremendous pace, though other towns were slow to grow. English, French and Dutch tradesmen, whose immigration was encouraged, brought with them an interest in stylish, well-designed belongings and interior decoration.

Many noblemen who had spent years in exile in France with King Charles were deeply influenced by Renaissance thinking. On their return to Ireland, they were appalled at the backwardness of the country, and most of them set about building mansions in the architectural styles familiar to them from France. The duke and duchess of Ormond rebuilt Kilkenny Castle, while many others reclaimed their estates and built afresh, leaving the medieval castle standing nearby or incorporating it into their new house.

Dublin expands

In Dublin, the small medieval town was too squalid to attract the followers of the vice-regal court, and new suburbs were created along Aungier Street, Thomas Street and Capel Street. St Stephen's Green was laid out in the 1660s. All of these new houses and mansions showed some measure of Renaissance proportion and a preoccupation with light. From the 1660s, windows in fashionable buildings were arranged in the orderly fashion necessary to proper classicism. Few designers had first-hand experience of Italy, and so they took their ideas from books, from the drawings of those who had seen Italy, and from pure imagination. Nevertheless, the results were definitely of the Renaissance school.

The Royal Hospital, Kilmainham, incorporated elements of classical detail and design never before combined in Ireland on such a huge scale. The rows of identical upright windows stretch into the distance, while to light the dining room, chapel and master's lodgings there are monumental arched windows, spanning two floors. Venerable though this building looks with its sedate sash windows, the original effect can only be guessed at, as until the mid-eighteenth century each window was divided into four lights by a mullion and transom, opening outwards to air the rooms. Each was fitted with small leaded squares of glass that would have glinted with countless reflections.

The Royal Hospital, Kilmainham

James Butler, first duke of Ormond and a close associate of King Charles II, was the greatest influence on the architecture of Ireland in this period. While he was viceroy, the face of Ireland became recognisably modern. One building for which he was responsible, the Royal Hospital in Kilmainham, changed Irish attitudes to architecture and windows for generations to come.

The Royal Hospital, built between 1680 and 1684, burst upon the consciousness of a public largely ignorant of classical design. Arranged on four sides of a courtyard, with large, classically positioned windows lighting airy rooms, it was the crowning achievement of its day. Suddenly, architects, owners and builders saw the benefits of building in this manner, and the style spread. From this point on, Irish architecture became classical architecture.

The introduction of sash windows

Although the Royal Hospital was not given sash windows until well into the eighteenth century, these distinctive, sliding, wooden-framed windows became fashionable from the 1680s on—the duke of Ormond used them at Kilkenny Castle in 1680. Very soon, the sash window was an indispensable element in new Irish architecture—a position it retained until the middle of this century.

Most of the buildings of Ireland were new in the early eighteenth century, and an English visitor, John Loveday, was struck in 1732 by the number of sash windows he saw. 'Even thatched houses are sash'd in Ireland', he wrote.

As well as providing more light, these windows looked better in that they consisted of an ordered grid on the classically arranged façade. Instead of a dark mix of lead lines and a bulky mullion and transom, the sashes echoed the classical preoccupation with rectangles. Sashes were often painted a light 'stone' colour to show off their contribution to the overall design of the building.

Technical refinements

Practical improvements helped to bring about changes in the details of windows. During the first half of the eighteenth century very correct proportions based on Palladio's principles were in vogue. Houses in Henrietta Street, Dublin, were built with very widely spaced windows. This followed

Window joinery and glass-making reached a very fine standard in the late eighteenth century. Sashes were fashioned with ever-thinner glazing bars, the most slender being made of metal. Glass-making skills were honed to such a degree that the flat 'crowns' were paper-thin, spun to a diameter of about five feet across. The public demanded improvements in glass and joinery in the quest for more light and an uninterrupted view of the landscape. The result, seen here in North Great George's Street, Dublin, was perfection, but not mere mechanical precision. Old glass always displays signs of its manufacture—curves in crown glass, shimmering bumps in cylinder sheet glass.

When the sun shines on the red brick squares of Dublin it dances on the irregular crown and sheet glass surfaces, and the white 'patent' reveals (sides of the window opening) catch the light and reflect it inwards and outwards, as seen in Upper Mount Street. From the exterior there is a dazzling effect, outlining all the windows on the street, measuring the length of each. Upper Mount Street was developed piecemeal, but each group of houses conformed to an overall pattern informed as much by classical tradition as by legislation.

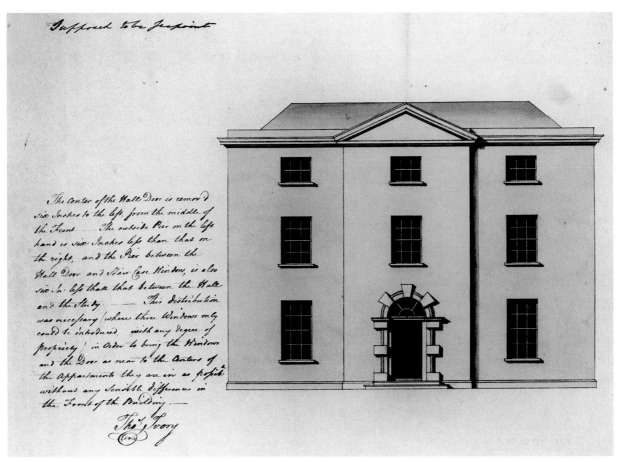

It is unusual to find a middle-sized house like this drawn out by an architect, and rarer still to read an explanation for its proportions such as is found in the small script beside this illustration. Thomas Ivory, the architect, was concerned that his patron, Lord Belmore, should understand that he had to place some of the windows nearer to each other than usual in order to achieve a properly classical result from both inside and outside. Such attention demonstrates how important fenestration had become by the second half of the eighteenth century. Ivory also drew in the glazing bars, not commonly done at this time, which makes the house easier to visualise.

Italian taste without the Italian sunshine, so windows were gradually modified to better suit our climate. In the windows of these decades the sashes had thick glazing bars, usually two inches wide, and each sash would have at least six panes, and often nine or twelve. This made the window very prominent in the front of the building. These early windows were usually set very close to the face of the wall, with visible frames. However, an act passed in 1730 decreed that they should be set back for the width of one brick into the reveal, and this gradually became standard.

By the 1750s there was a push for change from the very thickly gridded window to a more refined profile with larger panes of glass. As interest grew in both indoor activities, such as reading, and outdoor planting and landscaping, it became obvious that the window would have to be slimmed down. Mrs Delany, a friend of Dean Swift, admired the new fashion and in 1759 ordered sashes 'new made in the narrow way, which makes them much pleasanter'.

Because the influence of proportion was so strong, it was not really feasible to enlarge the window. So, along with the thinner profile, the frame holding the weights, which had obstructed several inches all round, was now hidden in the wall, giving a more refined appearance (and also helping to protect the timber from damp).

The Wide Streets Commissioners

By the 1760s, very little deviation from the rules of classical architecture was permitted in fashionable buildings. When the Wide Streets Commissioners began to rebuild and expand Dublin, they were interested in regulating proportion according to the latest taste, and favoured uniformity along the streetscape. One unfortunate builder was ordered to lower his windows by four inches to satisfy them. Similarly, in Cork the City Corporation ordered a group of builders in a particular street to have the windows of their houses ranged like those of Mr Shaw, who presumably had built the first house in that terrace.

The Commissioners ruled in Dublin that no wooden doorcases and no jutting-out (i.e. bay or oriel) windows were permitted. As a result, a distinctly Dublin style of Georgian house evolved, bare of ornamentation apart from the strictly positioned windows and a stone doorcase, usually with fanlight and columns.

Often an interesting history is hidden behind odd or non-classical fenestration. As this house is in Kilkenny, it is quite likely that the windows we see here were later modifications to a medieval building. The large gap between the first and second floors supports the possibility that the façade was altered. Perhaps originally there were gables facing the street, and the front wall was built up owing to difficulties with maintenance. The neighbouring houses are similarly proportioned, but to a different scale and more rigidly classical. Houses like McGrath's are usually good subjects for historical research—it is surprising how much information can be contained in the fenestration.

This residential shop on a prominent site in Kinsale is charming but not typically Irish. It is unusual in that the roof is laid front to back, with one large front gable. However, within these non-classical limits, the designer achieved good proportions and symmetry in the windows and shop front. It is very well kept and a great advertisement both for old houses in general and for Kinsale.

Georgian flowering

In the second half of the eighteenth century, Irish architecture participated fully in the flowering of the arts that was transforming the atmosphere in the whole country, helping to establish a feeling of national pride. The Customs Houses in Limerick and Dublin and the squares and crescents of the Georgian cities elicited approval from the inhabitants and wonder from visitors.

By now, more landowners and tradespeople than ever were in a position to build. There was a general rise in the standard of living, and the middle and artisan classes prospered. Books of house design and architectural details, as well as builders' guides, helped to circulate the latest fashions, not only for the big house but also for farms and rural smallholdings.

The Window Tax, enforced in England in 1695, was not imposed here until 1799. It undoubtedly affected the purse of the property-holder, but there is not much evidence that fewer windows were inserted (or windows blocked up) to lessen liability. Sometimes blind windows were inserted to suit the overall appearance where it would be inconvenient to have a window on the inside. The Window Tax was repealed in 1851 after years of lobbying.

Not all of the classical rules were adhered to, nor were all windows graded in size. These differences lend charm and personality to the buildings of Ireland. In towns, the use of plots of various widths meant that buildings on a street were slightly differently scaled, and this increases their attractiveness. The more practical builders, less preoccupied with ideals, often placed the door and ground-floor windows off-centre, rather than lining them up with the windows of the other floors.

Peasant houses

A visitor to rural Ireland in the 1770s, Mark Elstob, described the tenant farmworkers' houses as having a chimney (or a hole in the roof) and 'a window of about a foot square in the front, and a whited outside, in imitation of their tyrannic Lord's'. The windows of these houses were not used for the purposes of admiring a well-groomed landscape but for providing a modicum of daylight. Most windows were shuttered for security and heat conservation. At the most basic level, the kitchen table doubled as a shutter, hinging up to cover the window at night.

The tiny windows described by Elstob were not suitable for sashes. Instead, the cheapest glass was glazed into a simple frame, which might be hinged at the side or just left fixed. When even offcuts of glass were too expensive, rags and boards were used.

Many of our stock of solid rural houses, mostly farmhouses, were put up by landlords for their tenants. According to the imagination and financial inclination of the owner, much understated style, in the best classical taste, was designed into these unpretentious buildings.

This rubble stone, thatched Sligo cottage may be small and humble, but almost hidden in the thick wall are two tiny sash windows. They were probably the most expensive item in the construction of the house, and signify a level of architectural, fashion and social awareness that belies their surroundings. They recall John Loveday's comment of 1732 that 'even thatched houses are sash'd in Ireland'.

Egmount Place, Kanturk.

3. CHANGE AND INNOVATION— THE VICTORIAN ERA

The nineteenth century begins

Most provincial Irish towns and cities are products of the early nineteenth century. Despite growing poverty, dissent and finally rebellion, followed by the Act of Union, no obvious stylistic changes are visible between the buildings of the 1790s and those erected for a number of years after 1800. The positioning of the windows followed the usual classical lines. Very little surface decoration was used, resulting in understated houses with perhaps only a bow window or a few semicircular arched windows as external decoration. The columnated doorcase was used all over the country, and the fanlight sometimes grew to a massive size, encompassing the door and a pair of fat sidelights.

Interest in pre-Renaissance styles of building became widespread with the new century, and 'Gothic' and 'Tudor' details were intertwined with the classical format, often embellishing gatelodges and almshouses, such as those in Castle Bellingham and Tallow (see illustrations on pp 42 and 44).

The Victorian era

The Victorian era brought change, innovation and architectural revivals which finally eclipsed the classical style. The Gothic Revival became so popular that, by the mid-century, it began to seriously rival the classical. By the 1860s they coexisted, each borrowing elements of window design from the other.

Closely associated with Gothic was the Tudor style, a rehash of the architecture of sixteenth-century England. By using Gothic or Tudor styles, the architect gained the freedom to punch windows wherever he thought suitable. Moreover, they could be any size he wished, to better fit small and large rooms alike, without all having to line up on the outside.

Castles, gatelodges, churches and the new railway buildings were all favourite targets for the highly decorative Tudor/Gothic treatment. They were given battlements, porches with finials, huge medieval chimney-pieces, and, everywhere, the mullioned window.

The gracious terrace of houses on Grand Parade, Cork, derives much of its elegance from the tall, slate-hung bow fronts. The wide use of bow windows and slate-hanging, seen here, is a feature of southern counties. The windows are very wide, so to avoid breaking the rules of classical design they are divided into three tall sashes. In many old bow windows the sashes are curved, which (see diagram, p. 73) was a job requiring skill and finesse. The sashes in this house are modern, proving that joiners today are just as capable of producing first-class work; some, however, have been replaced by flat sashes, which appear stilted.

In the eighteenth and nineteenth centuries there was a long-lasting fashion for a touch of Gothic, such as little pointed arches in what were essentially classical buildings. This terraced house and shop in Youghal is a perfect (and probably overlooked) example of such picturesque work, which fortunately has survived while many more like it have been replaced without a thought. The result is visually very pleasing and a tribute to the input of either designer or owner. These windows are a minor treasure, unique in Youghal, and deserving of continued appreciation and maintenance.

(Left) There are many small buildings around the country which, although designed by architects, were not embellished with major 'features'. Tallow Almshouse (1830) is one such unassuming building, which relies entirely on fenestration and projecting porches for visual effect. The designer was obviously concerned with aesthetics as well as function, however, as these Tudor Revival windows were then the height of fashion. Wide windows were always divided vertically; here the arched lights and timber mullions are simple but pleasing. Casement windows were considered appropriate for humble buildings (grander architecture was almost invariably given sash windows).

At Castle Bellingham, Co. Louth, the estate cottages of the 1830s, built in the era of the Picturesque, consciously avoid all signs of classical fenestration. They have windows placed where convenient to the plan and of various types—arched heads, Tudor oriels and dormers. The sash window was rejected in favour of the appropriately rustic casement type. Such picturesque cottages were built by the hundred, not only to house the workers (who could have been accommodated plainly) but to beautify villages and estates.

Gothic windows

The window was very easy to convert to a Gothic style. The sash was obviously classical, so what better way to break with tradition than to revive the mullioned and transomed medieval window? The whole arrangement was topped with stone or stucco hood-moulds. This gave a distinctly different air to a building, even if its elevations and plan were still essentially classical.

Cast-iron windows

Cast-iron windows were the product of new manufacturing methods. It was thought that the new material would require less maintenance, although that has not always proved correct. Cast-iron windows were not often used in upper-class homes, although some castles, such as at Malahide, Co. Dublin, went straight from medieval leaded windows to cast-iron quarry windows of the same appearance. Almshouses and gatelodges were also fitted with these windows, presumably for reasons of economy. One remarkable surviving crescent of cottages, in Raheny, Dublin, still have their pointed-arched, cast-iron quarry windows, which pivot open about their central axis (see p. 48).

New styles emerge

The hallmark of the Victorian period was a readiness to accept almost any architectural style. The ethos of proportion and restraint was no longer dominant, and it showed in the windows of many provincial towns. Towards the end of the century in particular, Hiberno-Romanesque details decorated large-paned Victorian sash windows, while in many places cast-iron quarry lights were fitted into sashes. Arched windows, many with very shallow curved arches, were again in vogue.

Decoratively treated windows are found in many late Victorian classical houses, and there was a fashion in the Listowel area for wonderful plasterwork to dress quite ordinary sash windows.

Stained glass was avidly adopted in domestic houses, and many still have coloured leaded glass in the top sections of the windows. Stained and leaded glass is often found around the doorcase, as well as in the top two panels of the door.

During the nineteenth century, cast-iron windows with a diamond pattern edged with a narrow border were very popular in churches; decorative cast iron could be formed easily and inexpensively. The very simple lancet windows here are in keeping with the small size of this Wexford church, and the lacy pattern adds considerable texture to the building.

Early this century Listowel and its hinterland benefited immeasurably from the artistic individualism of a family of stuccodores, whose work is exemplified in this cheerful architrave decoration. Very often both designer and owner ignore the upper floors of our town buildings, but wonderful exceptions such as Con Dillon's pub remind us that windows can be the focal point of ordinary street architecture. This splendid design is bright and exotic enough to have been transplanted from a Mediterranean port; it is a house of which all Listowel can be proud.

(Left) A good designer can produce beauty out of the most ordinary ingredients. In architecture simplicity and repetition are often the key, as in classical fenestration. The designer of Foley's in Lismore achieved a distinctive and effective façade by using just the basic arched window and little else. He carefully modulated the three openings to line up the shop front with the upper-floor windows, but positioned the doorway so that the distance between the windows and door is the same width as the door itself. All of the arches line up, even though the window arches are slightly wider than the door, and a simple plat band unites them all at the spring of each arch. It is a masterfully understated composition.

(Above) In the last years of the nineteenth century thousands of terraced houses were built for the new middle classes. Many of these had a canted (or angled) bay window, which remained popular until the Second World War. It pushed the drawing room out into the garden, giving more light and a feeling of spaciousness. Canted bay windows were fitted onto many existing houses too, such as this one in Fethard, which was given two, as befitted a sizeable town house. Note the 'horns', found on most sashes from the mid-nineteenth century onwards.

(Top left) While many mansions and castles were built using the 'latest' Gothic details, fewer cottages were designed with such attention to fashion. Here in Raheny is a rare survival, a crescent of estate cottages complete with original Gothic cast-iron arched windows, which swivel open about the central axis. All over Ireland small foundries produced cast-iron windows in imitation of leaded lights with diamond-shaped panes (or quarries), equally suited to castle, church and cottage.

(Bottom left) The Cigar Divan in Carlow must be one of the most beautifully proportioned shop fronts in Ireland, with its four graceful arches—three in the large-paned display window and the fourth over the door. Its design is timeless, but a hint of the period can be seen in the decorative grille under the window—pure art nouveau. The windows are as large and clear as money could buy, with slim but strong wooden glazing bars. Shop fronts like this are rare indeed, and should be valued. They seem priceless by comparison with the rash of ill-proportioned modern 'traditional' shop fronts that are replacing them.

This terrace of RIC dwellings in Castlecomer was inspired by the Arts and Crafts movement, which rejected classicism; here the windows are obviously designed for the convenience of the rooms rather than for regimentation (forgive the pun) on the façade. The casement windows suit the small openings; sashes were avoided in small houses around the turn of the century, especially by Arts and Crafts aficionados, because of their links with classicism. However, although the intention was modern, the windows are similar to old-fashioned casements with small panes.

Bay windows

It became increasingly common in larger middle-class houses to enhance the ground floor with projecting bay windows. Old houses could be brought up to date by the use of bay windows. At Fethard, two canted bay windows were fitted onto an earlier town house that otherwise has the usual classical arrangement. Despite the popularity of bay windows for bright living rooms, most windows, whatever the type, were designed to fit the perennial vertical rectangle.

New technology

New technology, in the shape of large sheets of glass developed in the early nineteenth century, had a profound effect on Irish buildings. Not only were huge shop display windows now feasible, but domestic sashes were modernised by removal of the glazing bars, giving a clearer view of the world and more indoor light. In order to reinforce these heavier windows, the corner joints were strengthened by the addition of 'horns'. With typical Victorian overstatement, horns were embellished using curved shapes. (Eighteenth-century sashes never have horns.)

New types of window were adopted, both with and without glazing bars. Mass-produced, illustrated builders' catalogues, which advertised different types of windows, replaced the old architectural pattern books. As well as the sash and the cast-iron quarry light, one could have the popular French window, which stretched from floor to ceiling. There were pivoting windows and hopper windows, which were hinged on the bottom rail, often employed over a normal sash. Another new type opened outwards and was hinged on the top rail. This is now found universally, often in large unwieldy sizes in modern windows. The combination window became very popular at the end of the nineteenth century—two side-hung casements surmounted by a top-hung casement.

The humble window was taken more and more out of the sphere of the local joiner and into the area of mass production. The spread of industrialised components, usually patented, for hinging, opening, locking and balancing windows was quite extraordinary. Many Irish manufacturers produced their own versions of foreign innovations for the expanding house market.

By the middle of this century, glass-making was completely automated, allowing windows of any size to be designed. This freedom to think on a large scale changed the face of architecture worldwide. Improvements in reinforced

By the close of the nineteenth century builders' suppliers were huge concerns, turning out windows and doors by the thousand for the new terraced suburbs. W. & L. Crowe Ltd, of Dublin, was one such firm which imported timber and had its own sawmills. Its catalogue (right and below) details the standard window cross-sections and appearance, using redwood and red deal for sashes and frames. The segmentally headed sash window was quite common in Dublin at the turn of the century—such refinements were always somewhat more expensive but nonetheless very popular.

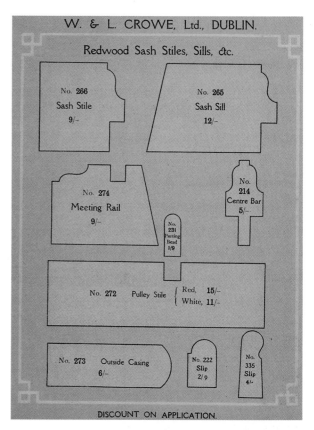

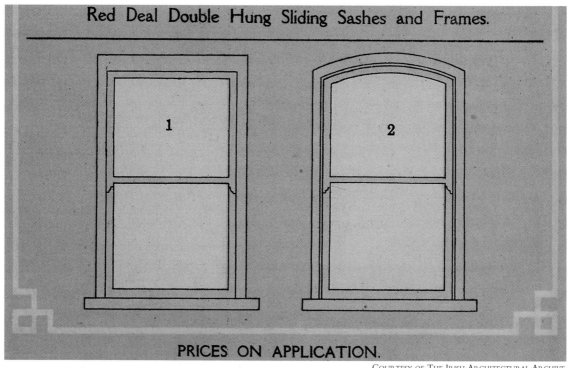

COURTESY OF THE IRISH ARCHITECTURAL ARCHIVE

concrete construction enabled these huge windows to effectively cloak the whole building, and curtain walls were born.

Modern movement

While ordinary people were enthusiastic about the various revivals of style, the modernists, notably the Bauhaus Movement in Germany between 1910 and 1920, felt that it was time to design buildings for the modern age. The modern movement adopted the principle of 'form follows function'—in other words, the use of a building determined the form, type and position of the windows. In a reaction to the tall window of old, horizontal rectangles were widely used. Out went the sash and most types of timber window, and in came the mass-produced steel window, with a sleek profile and the capacity to be tailored to any requirement. Function, with little reference to past architectural principles, ruled the modernists. These designers had little time for embellishment, arguing that beauty arose from the simplicity of use and purpose.

In Ireland, this approach to architecture did not become popular. A number of very stark, white-painted houses with flat roofs and horizontal steel casement windows were built which challenged the accepted ideals. Several of these ground-breaking buildings, with wrap-around windows using the latest in glass technology, still exist. However, the ordinary Irish house was conservatively styled and relied on all manner of borrowed themes, shown most readily in an eclectic window design.

This push and pull between old and new, between comfortable notions of the past and excited dreams of progress, continues as ever. Only time will tell whether the modern window will also leave a legacy for the interest of future viewers equal to that of the classical era.

Fethard, Co. Tipperary.

4. KNOW YOUR GLASS—IDENTIFYING OLD GLASS BY ITS APPEARANCE

In former times, glass was made by highly specialised craftsmen. Almost all original glass that survives in eighteenth- and nineteenth-century windows was fashioned by glass-blowers who used a method similar to that still employed by crystal glass-makers today.

Old panes of glass have an individuality that is the result of how they were blown, of how the molten glass was melted and stirred, and of the variation in and quality of the ingredients. Various tints of colour can be seen, formed over the years by light acting on chemicals in the glass. Purple and green are the most common colours—green from too much iron in the sand, and purple from manganese added to the mix to prevent a greenish tint from forming in the first place.

In the making of glass, air bubbles can easily form. In crown glass they are usually round, while cylinder glass has elongated bubbles. Occasionally the surface is blemished by bumps because molten glass is syrupy and if any other bits of glass or dirt hit it they will attach themselves.

Because of colour or surface faults, different qualities of glass were sold. The best was clear and even, free from colour, surface imperfections and warp. It is said that this ideal quality was rarely reached, but several Irish glasshouses advertised their first-quality crown, and many panes of crown glass that survive are of that superior quality.

Look closely at old panes of glass and the surface patterns will tell you how it was made.

Cylinder glass

Irregular dents and bumps in the surface characterise 'cylinder sheet' glass (see opposite). Broad cylinder glass is made from a hollow blown cylinder of glass which is opened out into discs or sheets while the glass is still almost molten. The cylinder was cut open along its length and then eased open and flattened on a sanded table with a wooden tool. This was also known as 'muff' glass. As the glass was pressed against the flat table when it was still hot, it picked up an

DIDEROT'S *ENCYCLOPÉDIE*, 1762–77, VOL. IV, PLATE 34. COURTESY OF DOVER PUBLICATIONS

ILLUSTRATED LONDON NEWS 1852

Broad glass was made by blowing a bubble, lengthening it into a cylinder, and then, while still red hot, cutting it open along its length and flattening down the two sides into a sheet of glass. This glass was often warped and marked by the flattener; it was usually tinted green or yellowish and the clarity was far from perfect. A more streamlined method of production was developed in England in the 1830s and quickly became popular in Ireland. In this improved method there were fewer blemishes; longer cylinders were blown, and these were left to cool slowly (as all glass must) before being reheated and cut into large sheets.

DIDEROT'S ENCYCLOPÉDIE, 1762–77, VOL. X, PLATE 15. COURTESY OF DOVER PUBLICATIONS

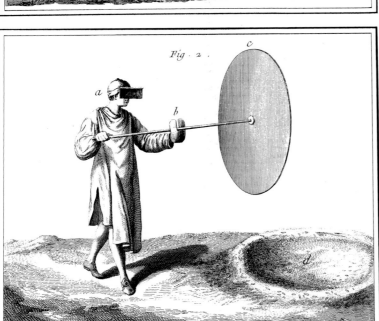

Crown or spun glass was for centuries the most sought-after type of window glass. A crown is a blown disc of glass, formed by blowing a globe and, by several delicate stages, opening it out at one end and 'flashing' it into a flat disc—while being rotated it unfurls like an umbrella. As each crown was made separately, all were different. However, slight rippling curves are visible in most of them. Many panes are slightly greenish, a result of the percentage of iron in the mix (common in sand, the basic ingredient of glass). Making crown glass was a very skilled process and the workmen were well paid, although subject to hazards in the course of the work.

NESSA ROCHE

As old glass was blown by hand, each pane 'throws' light differently, clearly seen when raking sunlight makes shadows of it. Crown glass has distinct concentric lines like the rippled waves formed when a drop reverberates on water. Cylinder sheet glass has a 'hammered' surface, without direction to the undulations. Seen as shadows, each type is distinct. (Float glass, free from imperfections, doesn't catch sunlight at all.)

image of the sanded metal surface, with indents, marks from the flattening tool and the occasional bit of dirt. Broad glass, therefore, was not highly transparent and was of a poorer quality than later types.

This process underwent constant refinement in Continental glasshouses during the eighteenth century, and improved cylinder glass, introduced into England in 1832, was based upon these better techniques, in which the cylinders were a good deal larger—five or six feet long. These large cylinders were allowed to cool, and were then reheated to a lower temperature in order to be cut and laid flat. Sheets of glass made by this method were superior in quality to earlier broad glass and became very popular in the mid- and late nineteenth century. The widespread adoption of improved cylinder glass owed more to the greater pane sizes obtainable than to its appearance, which was often criticised for its erratic surface imperfections.

Crown glass

Crown glass was originally made in Normandy, France, but the process was introduced to Ireland through London. The name 'crown' refers to the maker's mark—a crown—used in the 1680s by the first English glasshouse to produce these discs.

Crown glass manufacture involved blowing a small bubble on a long metal blowpipe to the size of a large globe. It was then transferred to another rod and widened into a large U-shaped bowl, and finally 'flashed' or spun so fast that it flattened out into a disc. This was a highly skilled process.

The circular shape caused the rings which are found in crown glass window panes. At the centre of the disc was the bull's-eye or bullion. It was thicker and had an extra glob of glass on it where it was cracked off the iron rod. The bullion was usually rough—some bullions are still sharp after several hundred years. Crown glass was 'heat-polished'—that is, the surfaces were softened by heat and did not touch anything else while still hot. The quality and luminosity of this glass, at its best almost free of any curves, made it prized for centuries as the best affordable material.

Polished plate glass

In polished plate glass the surface is almost flawless and has a rich sheen. Panes

DIDEROT'S *ENCYCLOPÉDIE*, 1762–77, VOL. IV, PLATE 24, AND VOL. VIII, PLATE 1. COURTESY OF DOVER PUBLICATIONS

Cast plate glass, as shown here in two eighteenth-century engravings, was produced by melting glass in a crucible and pouring it onto a large metal plate. The molten glass was then rolled flat and slowly cooled down. When cold, both sides had to be ground and polished until they shone flat and clear. By the end of the eighteenth century steam engines assisted in the polishing, but the work was still difficult and time-consuming. The whole process was fraught with many hazards, which meant that cast plate glass was extremely expensive. However, the large sizes enabled the richest people to have windows with no glazing bars, and so plate glass windows gave a house a certain cachet.

of this type are only rarely seen—it was most often used for mirrors.

Polished plate glass could be made by two methods. The older one was to blow thicker crown discs or cylinders, while the French invented a method of casting glass plates in the 1680s. In order to achieve the smoothest surface, both sides of the blown or cast glass plate were ground flat using sand, and polished to a high sheen using emery and rouge. The success of an English cast plate manufactory and the invention of glass-grinding machinery helped this glass to become more readily available in the nineteenth century, although still expensive.

Old cast plate glass often has swirls in it, but otherwise is hard to identify.

Patent plate glass

Patent plate glass is a polished sheet glass made by the improved cylinder sheet method. It was blown and then ground and polished in a partly mechanised process patented in 1838, producing fewer bumps and lumps. Panes of this glass are not as flat as cast plate but they have a sheen not found on ordinary cylinder panes arising from the polished surfaces.

Drawn glass

Glass panes that have parallel lines or streaks running across the surface like music notation lines have been made by the early twentieth-century 'drawn' process. Various automated glass-making processes competed with each other until the 1950s, when another revolutionary method bypassed them all. Float glass is made by casting glass onto an enormous plate of molten tin which repels the glass, in effect polishing it on contact. The finished sheet emerges with both sides of the glass polished, of a standard unvarying width and absolutely free of imperfections.

Model Arts Centre, Sligo.

5. WINDOW CRAFTSMEN: GLASS-MAKING AND GLASS-MAKERS, GLAZIERS AND JOINERS

The prospect of profit from turning ordinary sand, lime and kelp into expensive glass encouraged a number of the Anglo-Irish gentry and planters to sponsor glasshouses during the seventeenth century, but it was a risk-filled business. The earl of Cork patronised a glasshouse on the border between Cork and Waterford in the 1620s, while at the same time Lord Rosse in Birr brought over the Bigo family of glass-makers from France. The Percivals in County Cork and Viscount Conway in Antrim also investigated setting up glasshouses later in the century.

In the eighteenth century, glass-making became more of an urban business. Fuel was by far the most expensive item on the glass-maker's bill. In the sixteenth and seventeenth centuries, timber was used. However, from the late seventeenth century onward, hotter, more efficient, coal-fired furnaces were invented, and these had to be located near the source of the fuel, or by a port.

In the seventeenth century all Irish glasshouses made broad cylinder glass, but in the eighteenth century crown glass began to be produced at a little-recorded glasshouse outside Waterford City, which apparently was working by 1711. The more expensive crown glass found a ready market here, although much broad and crown glass was imported from England and the Continent.

In small towns, owing to the expense, demand was not always high. Glass became even more expensive if it had to be transported from the glasshouse or port. Carriage overland was treacherous, but if the glass was sent by boat it was liable to other hazards and delays. Letters survive from a Belfast merchant in the 1670s, when Belfast was still in its infancy, lamenting the slow sale of glass which he had had shipped from Dublin. The few cases he had bought were still not sold six months later, as local glaziers were refusing to pay the asking price.

However, in every period there was a market for window glass. The more expensive crown glass was used all over Ireland by those who could afford it. The select few even glazed their important windows with polished plate glass, which cost a fortune. In the nineteenth century plate glass windows were still so expensive that they were sometimes insured separately against damage. Even in a slow economy glass regularly needs replacement, and accounts survive that detail endless repairs. Before timber windows became common the rate of breakage was far higher, as leaded windows were susceptible to destruction in storms.

Belfaſt Glaſs Manufactory.

BENJAMIN EDWARDS, at his FLINT GLASS-WORKS in Belfaſt, has now made, and is conſtantly mak-ing all Kinds of enamell'd, cut, and plain Wine Glaſſes; cut and plain Decanters with Flint Stoppers; Crofts; com-mon, Dram, and Punch Glaſ-ſes; Flint and green Phials; Flint and Green Guarde du-Vin; Retorts; Receivers, and all Manner of Kinds of Chymical Ware; Cruets, Salts, and Goblets, &c. &c. &c.

The above FACTORY has been compleated at a very conſiderable Expence, and is equal to any in England; and as there are vaſt Quantities of Goods of all Sorts now on Hands, Cuſtomers cannot poſſi-bly be diſappointed.

The Proprietor has brought a GLASS CUTTER from England, who is conſtantly employed, and humbly hopes for the Protection and Countenance of all the Friends of Ireland, to pleaſe whom, and to merit the Continuance of their Favours, which he has already received, ſhall be his conſtant Stu-dy.——Country Dealers will be ſuppl ed on the moſt reaſonable Terms.

Belfaſt Jan. 8th, 1781.

Eighteenth- and nineteenth-century glasshouses in Ireland (and England) were cone-shaped brick buildings. They were large features on the landscape, usually belching smoke, with fires and ovens at the base, around which teams of glass-blowers worked. A few years after this advertisement of 1781, Benjamin Edwards's glasshouse was dwarfed by a new neighbouring cone, the window-glasshouse of Smylie and Company, the largest in the British Isles, standing about 120ft high. Glass-making was an esoteric occupation and attracted visits from the curious, who marvelled that such a delicate product could emanate from such hot and dangerous work. Glass-makers were regarded as clannish; they were well paid but prone to drink and usually died young.

Pitfalls

Glass-making was a difficult enterprise and many pitfalls could destroy the business. A lot of money had to be invested for several years before there was any chance of recouping it. The glass-makers had to be paid from the day they were hired to prevent them from leaving before the furnaces were ready to melt the glass, and they commanded unheard-of wages. They were also paid for every day they were idle, for example when the furnace was cooled down because a pot was broken or for necessary maintenance.

Glasshouses themselves, built of brick, often faced structural problems. They were specialised buildings to erect, and several in eighteenth-century Dublin proved to be unsound, falling and killing workers and passers-by.

The ceramic pots in which the glass mix was melted were liable to crack when hot, and a whole batch of melted glass and much time and expense would be lost. If the mix was not right, or not heated to the correct temperature for long enough, which was difficult to gauge when using coal or wood fires, then the finished glass would be inferior, even unsaleable.

The skill of the blowers and their teams was vital to success. It was desirable to make large, clear, flawless crowns and cylinders, but many were inferior and so, for the same capital and running expenses, the glass fetched a lower price. Even quarrelling and sabotage were likely to occur among the workers, who appear (from reports and petitions) to have been constantly threatening to leave.

When glass was being made, the glasshouse worked around the clock. The teams were paid bonuses, often amounting to double their salaries, for producing more than the specified weekly output. To further sweeten them, some firms provided free accommodation. There was an outcry among glass-makers in England in 1745 when the new glass tax was seen as a threat to their livelihood. This necessitated the presence in the glasshouse, day and night, of excise officers whose job it was to calculate whether or not the owner was trying to cheat the revenue commissioners.

Because of the glass tax, many English glass-makers moved to Ireland after 1745, and worked successfully here for several generations. Their descendants, however, were put out of business by competition from larger British firms and by the introduction of the glass tax here in 1825. Despite many appeals and its obvious effect on light and health, the glass tax was not repealed until 1845.

The trade of glazing was not held in high esteem by architects, even though the glazier had to deal with extremely thin and delicate crown glass. This glazier has cut up the panes he requires, and has half a disc or crown of glass left over against the wall. Note the fanlight and other sashes awaiting glazing, leaning against the rough case with straw in which the crowns of glass were transported from the glasshouse. In his mouth the glazier has his glass-cutter, which held a diamond. Diamonds have always been used to cut glass; the sharp diamond scored the surface of the glass, which then cracked along the line when the glazier applied some pressure to the cut.

Glass-makers

The secrets of glass-making were usually passed on in families. One glass-making family named Bigo (from de Bigault) came to Ireland from France via England in 1623. Their name comes up several times over the course of the century as glass-makers in Offaly. The Bigos and the other Irish glass-makers of that era made broad cylinder glass, as they came from the Lorraine area, around the Rhineland, which had this tradition of glass-making. A member of another established Lorraine glass-making family, de Hennezell or Henzy, arrived in Leix in the 1660s and seems to have had some success in producing glass.

Glass-makers were fiercely tribal and rarely mixed with outsiders. In France they had been considered to be on a par with the lower echelons of the nobility, and all were acutely aware of their superior status among craftsmen. The prospect of very high wages and special status in foreign countries encouraged many Continental glass-makers to travel.

In the 1620s, the French glass-blower who made cylinder glass at a works in County Waterford struck a deal with the management whereby he received 54 shillings a week for a specified amount of glass. The wages earned by Normandy glass-makers in the 1580s in England stretched to eighteen shillings per day! In Belfast in 1832, bottle-makers, who commanded less money than window glass-makers, made five to six shillings per day.

For glass-makers, the drawbacks of their trade were the working conditions. 'Glassmakers generally drink a good deal and seldom live long', wrote the Rev. James Hall in 1813 of glass-makers in Cork. The atmosphere in and around the glasshouse was appallingly bad, with noxious fumes day and night. The *Dublin Journal* in 1770 described the fumes as 'cephalic', and again, in 1793, the editor called the glasshouses near the new Custom House 'abominable nuisances', spouting forth 'clouds of smoke that can only be likened to the discharges of thundering Etna'.

Several enterprises in Dublin, at Abbey Street backing onto Bachelor's Quay (the block now occupied by Wynn's Hotel) and at Marlborough Green (around the site of the Irish Life Centre), made crown glass until the end of the eighteenth century. Other Dublin works were at the North Wall and Ringsend. Crown glass was also made in Waterford at the start of the century, in Ballycastle, Co. Antrim, during the middle years, and in Belfast for about twenty years from the 1780s.

Increasing competition at the end of the eighteenth century, especially from Scottish glass-makers, forced them all out of business, although crown glass was

COURTESY OF DUBLIN CORPORATION (CITY ARCHIVES). PHOTOGRAPH BY HUGH MACCONVILLE

Occasionally a workman, owner or visitor inscribed their name and the date on a pane of glass, in an almost invisible attempt to gain immortality. It became a tradition for the craftsmen maintaining or repairing the dome of the Royal Exchange (now the City Hall) in Dublin to etch their names onto the glass of the dome. Neither Frazer nor Carton was enfranchised as a glazier in the Corporation Rolls. The exclamation probably reflected opposition to the new Custom House far to the east of the old city—and out of the control of the merchants who ran the Exchange.

made intermittently in Ringsend, Dublin, until the 1850s. Competition was ruthless. The Scottish firm Dumbarton was one of the main glassworks exporting to Ireland, and in the 1820s forced a Dublin maker out of business, apparently deliberately underselling him until he went bankrupt.

The repeal of the glass and window taxes, in 1845 and 1851 respectively, meant that prices fell dramatically. The small Irish enterprises failed to compete against much larger English and Scottish concerns, especially as these offered the new cylinder sheet glass which was made in larger sizes. This 'improved cylinder sheet glass', as its patenting firm, Chance Brothers of Birmingham, called it, gradually took over the market for glass in Ireland and forced other glass-makers out of business. It was never made here.

Glaziers

The brisk trade in window glass in the main towns allowed glaziers to make a healthy living. The Ringsend Crown Glass Company advertised its wares in the *Dublin Evening Post* of 1789, stating that they could be bought at the Window Glass Warehouse of John Raper on Lower Exchange Street, Dublin. Raper was a glazier by trade. He and his relatives, Thomas, Richard and William Raper, are good examples of successful craftsmen of their time. William, a glazier and wire lattice-maker, advertised that he had inherited his wife's shop in Dublin in 1766, carrying on a glazing and grocery business. In 1784 Richard Raper, glazier and grocer, was elected master of the Guild of St Loy (the Smiths' Guild). This was a prestigious position as the Smiths were third in importance only to the Merchants' and Tailors' Guilds.

John Raper's warehouse, opened in 1789, was separate from his house, the sign of a successful businessman at this time. He died in 1808, leaving property all over Dublin city to his widow Ann, including four new houses on Arran Quay and two on Gardiner Street which he had most probably built.

Not all glaziers were rewarded with financial success. Price rises, general hardship, extra import duties or perhaps a fire in the shop could put any craftsman out of business. Combining glazing with another trade helped to keep all the eggs out of one basket. Print-selling was a popular companion enterprise, as both dealt with window glass. George Meares, glazier and print-seller, went bankrupt in 1766 and petitioned Parliament to be freed from the debtors' prison. Painting and plumbing were also commonly attached to glazing, and perhaps also the grocery business, as carried on by the Rapers.

DIDEROT, *ENCYCLOPÉDIE*, 1762–77, VOL. VII, PL. 2. COURTESY OF DOVER PUBLICATIONS

Although the range of tools available to window-joiners expanded throughout the eighteenth century, enabling them to make sashes with very slender and elegant parts, machinery was basic. Often joiners transported themselves, their tools and the materials to each new job and made everything on site. (Many jobs were priced to include food and/or lodging.) Although some specialised in windows, most were competent in all types of finished woodwork. Indeed, by the mid-eighteenth century complete glazed sashes were sold off the shelf by shopkeepers such as the glazier and print-seller Thomas Silcock of Dublin, who advertised sashes of red deal glazed with Bristol crown glass at 12d per foot in 1751.

Glaziers set their prices according to a complicated scale, linked to the distance they had to travel to do the work (bringing the glass with them), the size of the panes cut and the quality of the glass. It was a system ripe for abuse, and at one stage the officials in charge of works at the Parliament House had to censure the contract glazier, John Rowlette, for overcharging them.

Joinery and joiners

Timber is the other constituent of the sash window. Developments in joinery are crucial to the history of windows, as styles always depended on what could be produced by joiners. As carpenters and joiners used refined joints in other work, it was a short step to applying their expertise to windows, and especially the sash window. Soon there were standard methods of making sashes, which survive to this day. Several types of joints requiring dexterity and special tools are necessary in making a sash window. As sashes became universal, tool-makers responded with appropriate tools for jobs such as forming the glazing bar profiles.

The earliest joiners in Ireland were probably English, coming here at the request of their employers, usually noblemen. But from very early on, Irish sash joiners were as skilled as the English, as affirmed in a letter from an agent to his employer in 1711: 'Assure yourself, that you will find as good of both kinds [carpenters and joiners] as you need desire, and I am sure cheaper, and more to your satisfaction'.

While sash-making methods soon became standard, the types of timber used varied according to suitability and cost. The most sought-after timber for house work was oak, but this was usually too expensive, and good, well-seasoned pine and fir proved to be lasting substitutes. Mahogany was used by the select few from the second half of the eighteenth century. Pine or fir was always painted while oak and mahogany were sometimes varnished, but the fashion for leaving softwoods unpainted is entirely modern.

Timber was imported into Ireland in vast quantities from Europe and later from America. By the time that timber windows became popular in the late seventeenth century, there were no forests left to speak of in the country. The use of superior wood, experience and sound joinery have helped old windows to survive for centuries. When repairs were necessary, joiners and carpenters knew methods that kept the windows sound for another hundred years or so. There was a continuity of craftsmanship that was broken only a generation ago, when the nature of apprenticeships changed.

COURTESY OF MICHAEL O'CONNELL

For the most part, Rock Cottage in County Antrim is unremarkable, but its startling gable window certainly lifts the house out of the ordinary. This octagonal opening could perhaps best be called 'carpenter's geometric'; it is a marvellous advertisement for its maker, who may have been a local man. The glazing bars are as carefully worked as the design; they are very finely moulded in typical late eighteenth-century style.

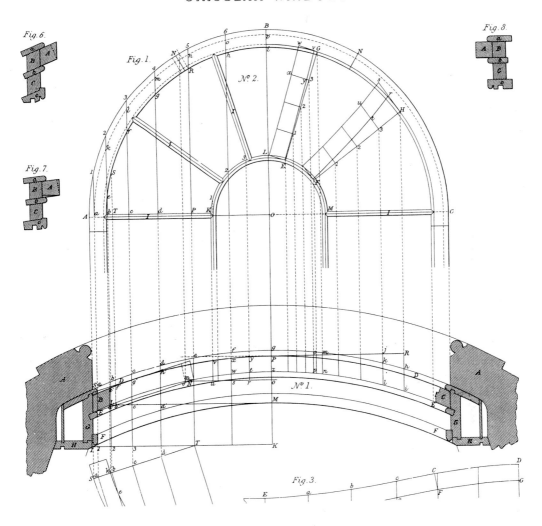

CIRCULAR WINDOW.

In the early nineteenth century illustrated instruction manuals started to appear, with fine engravings of the details necessary for the construction of windows (and other articles) of the best quality. As can be seen here, setting out a curved bow window with arched head was a complex matter, requiring the joiner to have a knowledge of geometry far beyond that which we associate with tradesmen today. It was generally agreed that window joinery was of a high standard; the Irish Builder *remarked in 1883 that it was clear that joiners of the Georgian period were skilled and interested in turning out well-finished and durable work.*

Tullow Street, Carlow.

6. CONTINUING THE TRADITION—KEEPING OLD WINDOWS ALIVE

Ordinary buildings in Ireland rely greatly for their beauty and ornamentation on the arrangement of their windows. These buildings, with their harmonious blend of windows and proportions, form the quietly attractive streets and towns that are a pleasing backdrop to our daily lives.

It is not just the shape of the windows that creates this visual harmony. It is the pleasantly aged timber and glass, the appearance of the sash or casement, the way the old glass catches and reflects the light, blending perfectly with mellowed old brick and stone, all gently rounded and softened by centuries of life, that together create the character of a building or street. There is no better example of this than the Old Library of Trinity College, Dublin, so praised by Maurice Craig (see Introduction, pp 1 and 4–5).

When this harmony is disturbed by inappropriate or intrusive shapes and materials, the entire streetscape is spoiled. A great deal of civic care and pride is lavished on our main streets and towns. But colourful plants, new paving and black and gold 'heritage' dustbins can't outweigh the eyesore presented by great numbers of clashing window types and materials, sticking out at all angles and breaking the line of the street façade.

The visual arguments for keeping old windows intact are obvious, but there are other reasons why it is important to conserve our historic timber windows.

Conservation

Conservation—literally good housekeeping—has always been a necessary part of life. Our ancestors couldn't afford to throw away perfectly good materials in exchange for a passing fad. But now enthusiasm for science and innovation, and the 'no maintenance' hard sell of advertising make it less easy to see that best value, in terms of money, buildings and health, still lies in ordinary maintenance.

The word 'conserve' means to preserve from decay or loss. Conservation does not mean replacing old windows with modern ones similar in design; it means care and repair. The intention of conservation is that the building should function as well as it was designed to.

There is no sight as alien to an Irish Georgian or Victorian terrace as rows of pro-truding factory-made windows, usually of aluminium or uPVC, sticking out at various angles. Whatever the social standing or size of an old building, uPVC is detrimental to both its visual appearance and its fabric. It is not good enough to cite a wish for 'maintenance-free' products: such a promise is a fallacy in any case. The damage done to the building—and to the health of the global community through the poisonous production and disposal of these items—long outlasts the short life of these inappropriate windows.

Moisture

Moisture is the main cause of Irish building problems. Rain, humidity, condensation and damp must all be taken into account when building and maintaining a structure. Because of our climate they can't be eliminated altogether, so we must live with them. People contribute enormous amounts of water just from normal living—gas heating, washing machines and bathing all increase moisture in our houses. Building materials must be able to 'breathe', to expand and contract with the weather, and to allow internal moisture to escape through the 'skin' of the building.

The health of both people and buildings requires a constant, low-level circulation of air. The increase in asthma and other breathing disorders has been linked to bad air quality indoors, caused when excessive sealing with unsuitable materials lessens the flow of air. (In the eighteenth and nineteenth centuries, a freshly aired house was called 'sweet', which is an apt description.) The stone, brick and timber of old buildings can 'breathe' in this fashion, while the parts of the structure are designed and built in a way that keeps the whole building healthy and air constantly circulating.

Trapped water

Modern alterations, such as installing uPVC or aluminium double-glazing, using hard plasters and sealing chimneys, all lessen the necessary flow of air and cause long-term damage to a building because water is trapped inside, setting up the ideal conditions for rot. The smell of damp often found in old houses, which often persuades the owner to install double-glazing, stems from a lack of air circulation, blocked gutters and faulty drainage. Fitting new, 'sealed' windows, especially of uPVC and aluminium, will worsen the problem, not cure it. (Of course, if they are made or fitted badly they will become a very expensive ventilation system in themselves!)

In repairing and maintaining buildings we need to work with the house, not against it. This means not tackling a problem in isolation—for example, trying to cure heat loss by installing uPVC windows. Quick-fix building solutions to address a specific problem often cause a side-effect elsewhere. Building products sold as being 'maintenance-free' are often seen as the answer, but regular, inexpensive care not only prevents costly problems but prolongs the life of all of the parts.

The simplest display window can be very effective, especially when it is well cared for, as in Gartland's in Kingscourt. These days paint or window boxes are often used to mask defects, but trouble will always flare up if the woodwork is neglected. Check behind window boxes periodically to ensure that damp does not build up on the sill and lead to future problems.

This early nineteenth-century terrace of houses on Capel Street in Dublin has Wyatt windows on all floors as the sites were too narrow to allow two ordinary windows. The unusual fenestration makes an interesting addition to the street. However, after years of neglect the fate of these three is uncertain; how should such buildings be restored? Is it acceptable to imitate their outline, replacing every bit of old material and calling it 'restoration'? In most 'modernisations', authenticity, period features and continuity are lost, and we gain yet another hotchpotch of modern materials and incorrect details pretending to be old while rejecting all that actually is old.

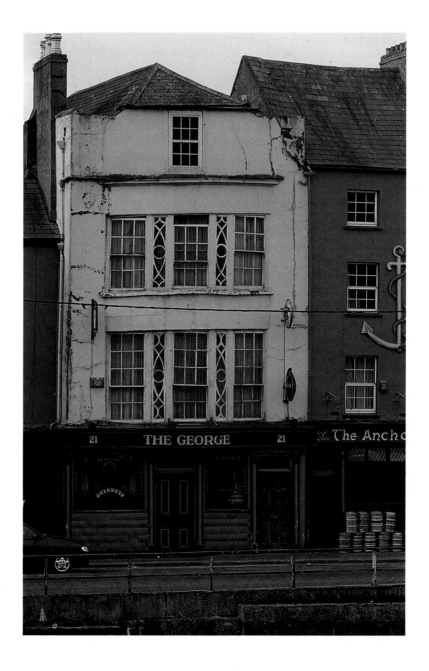

Some buildings in Cork are unlike any others in Ireland, with bow fronts and remarkable fenestration. The long, decoratively glazed windows between the sash windows are constructed with the techniques used by fanlight-makers and were probably made in Cork. These windows, and the house as a whole, deserve immediate help before there is any further deterioration—note that uPVC has already invaded the attic floor.

Money-saving

As long as windows function as they should, or can be repaired to do so, there is no practical or financial reason to remove them. The maintenance of windows saves money in the long term. Those that have been in place for decades—often centuries—represent by far the best guarantee of performance that anyone could need.

The design quality of old windows gives them a financial advantage. A properly crafted timber sash window is designed to fit in, proportionally, with the building. It is made of good timber, finely cut and planed. The sashes are moulded with a pleasing profile. The joints are solid, and the parts survive wear and tear remarkably well. If necessary, they can be taken apart and repaired.

Timber is the 'greenest' material there is. No huge chemical plants or steel or bauxite mills are required to grow it, and no rivers are polluted with its waste. What other material can be repaired so effectively as wood? What else can be adjusted, planed down or touched up? What else can be reused? What other materials have in-built defences against decay such as the resin in timber?

There are many ways to help to preserve windows and to upgrade them to meet modern living standards. If new parts or complete windows are required, they should match in all of their details. However, they will still be new items, only a substitute for the original.

Synthetic substitutes

How could a 20-year guarantee for uPVC compare with the proven success for 200 years of timber? Who knows whether the firm which offers a guarantee with its uPVC or aluminium double-glazed windows will still be around in 20 years to fulfil the promise? Aluminium and uPVC are expensive, and research shows that these so-called maintenance-free windows will commonly need replacement after about 30 years. Their hinges, catches and gaskets will not last even that long, and major repairs are impossible when damage is done.

And where do these windows go? To landfill, like most of Ireland's rubbish. However, the plastic and aluminium do not break down safely. They leach out their toxic elements into the groundwater, helping to pollute our country and our drinking water.

Then there is the eventual cost of replacing the worn-out windows. Buying cheap replacement windows is no saving—it is just a shorter route to the local

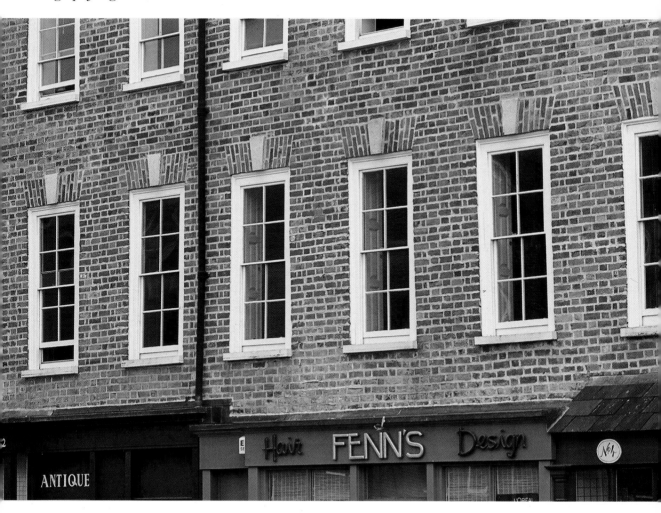

Sheare's Street in Cork (formerly Fenn's Quay), with its regularly spaced sash windows, displays all of the features of the ordinary Irish terrace of the mid-eighteenth century. These quite narrow windows have late eighteenth-century sashes divided in an uncommon pattern of four panes each. Until a few years ago the terrace looked forlorn and ripe for redevelopment. However, under enlightened guidance it has been restored, and a good deal of the window joinery kept—the joiner splicing in new timbers where necessary. Any surviving panelled shutters have also been kept (ideal for privacy and heat insulation), as have the window seats—convenient for watching life pass by outside.

dump. Every set of uPVC windows costs several thousand pounds. If these costs are calculated per year of life, they represent extremely bad value for the customer.

Double-glazing

Double-glazing, usual in replacement windows, is the least cost-effective method of energy-saving. You are unlikely to recoup the investment cost in the form of lower heating bills for 60 years. Only if windows *need* complete replacement (which rarely happens with old windows) is it economic to install double-glazing.

Lack of sound insulation is often used as an argument against old windows, but sound travels through all gaps in the house, not just the windows. Draught-proofing, a service offered by many joineries, counteracts noise pollution as much as is healthy for the occupants while allowing air to circulate. Responsible replacement window companies now insert vents into the windows which let sound in (and some heat out).

The installation of secondary glazing—separate inner windows—is a tried and tested way of cutting down on heating bills and improving sound insulation. When inserted in an unobtrusive design and material, they provide more sound and heat insulation than double-glazing and have little effect on the appearance of the house.

In recent years people have become more aware of the value of houses that still have their original fittings—intact fireplaces and internal doors. Taking out the original windows can actually reduce the value of an old house. Moreover, the resale value of a property with uPVC or aluminium windows rarely reflects the investment made in them, especially if the designs are ugly, unsuitable for the period or prove an obstacle to escape in the event of fire.

Montpelier Hill, Dublin.

7. *MAINTAINING AND IMPROVING YOUR SASH WINDOWS*

It is straightforward to identify troublespots and maintain a window, and joinery defects are well within the expertise of a good joiner or carpenter. Loose joints can be tightened, and areas where timber has decayed can be cut out and fitted with sound wood. There are particular areas to look out for, such as the bottom rails of the sashes, especially at the corners, and the sill and bottom of the frame, where they meet the stone sill. The piecing of new timber into the corners of the sash and frame is best left to a good joiner or carpenter, as the new joints must fit properly and must be cut so as to direct rainwater away from the putty and the interiors of the joints. Similarly, cutting out damaged sills can be done on site, but it requires expertise.

Paint and putty

The average householder could easily check the state of the putty and paint, and properly reputty and repaint when required. Paint has an effective life-span of up to ten years, but it should be reapplied every five years or so. Don't paint over flaking paint; instead, first sand it down (wearing a face-mask). Avoid using a heat gun as it may crack the glass. Putty should always be smooth on the outside so that rain runs off it. If it has broken into chunks, it allows moisture in to the glass and timber. Putty in this state is very easy to remove and replace. Only do the puttying when the timber is dry, and paint over it in a few weeks' time.

Sash pulleys

Another simple job is to check that the pulleys, cord and weights are working properly. Sash windows do get stuck, almost always because the cord breaks, the pulleys need oiling, or the sashes were painted into position. Sashes that are heavy to pull up or down have often been reglazed without having had the weights checked. Modern glass is heavier than crown or sheet glass, and as the

Maintaining a sash window by checking the condition of the paint and carrying out thorough repainting and rehanging is not beyond an ordinary householder's capabilities. Such tasks were once accepted as the necessary price of obtaining centuries of use from the window. Nowadays, with most people so busy, there is certainly an opening for enterprising glaziers, carpenters or joiners to set up maintenance companies to carry out such preventive conservation.

COURTESY OF IAN LUMLEY

Many urban terraces were designed with projecting bay windows. This most unusual example in Glasnevin, Dublin, is the full height of the house with its original sash windows intact—including a wonderful arched sash in the centre. There is no comparison between the visual appeal of this house and the replacement uPVC windows of its neighbours, with their thick lines and lights that protrude when open. Every week more of these unique original details are dumped in skips, to be replaced by anodyne and insensitively designed plastic, aluminium and timber replacements, without a thought for the wider picture.

weight of the glass accounts for about half the weight of the glazed sash, any increase in glass weight will affect how easily the sash can be moved.

If a joiner is not available to do this, unhook the cord and string heavy steel washers on it so that they rest on the weights. Make sure to check that the sash and both weights are balanced. A tip for easier operation is that the weights for the lower sash should be slightly lighter and those for the upper slightly heavier, the better to keep it up.

Draught-proofing

Air circulation is fine, but no one wants draughts in the house. A well-fitted window will admit the minimum air needed for the health of the house and its occupants. Patented draught-proofing systems are available in Ireland, made or imported by several companies. They cut down on air, but it should be stressed that a well-fitted window, operating as it was designed to do, should not need any extra help. Draught-proofing is most useful where constant use has worn the perimeters of the sashes, as the seals take up this slack.

A growing number of firms are now in the business of repairing and upgrading windows, as more and more people realise that the proven life of their house's original windows is the best guarantee of their future life expectancy. Financially, structurally and visually, the best course is to maintain and repair windows as necessary and hand them down intact to the next generation, and the one after that.

There may be trouble ahead

Some areas are susceptible to weathering in windows, whatever their framing material. Naturally, in a damp climate like that of Ireland, moisture is the biggest problem. Whereas most trouble spots were eliminated as far as was possible for the time, the areas where water can lie and permeate the timber should be checked periodically. The lower ends of the frame can soak in water, and if the stone sill is not sufficiently sloped this water may be slow to evaporate and may cause decay in the frame ends and/or timber sill. Where the timber is past saving, the ends of the frame can be cut away and new timbers spliced in — such work was always commonplace in the past. Fitting of new sills is also a routine job for a conservation joiner. The bottom rail, especially its lower

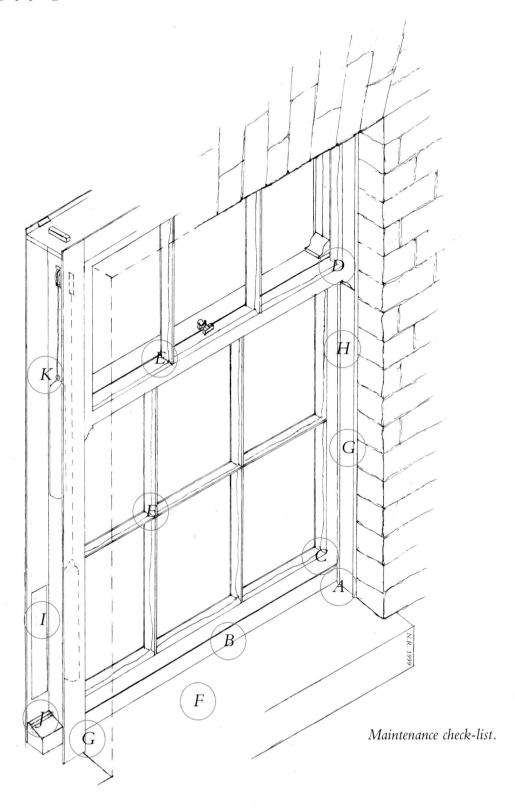

Maintenance check-list.

corners, is the main trouble spot in the sashes. Occasionally the meeting rail of the top sash also causes trouble, if the glazing bar joints are loose and the rail sags. Make sure that the paint and putty are still holding and the joints are tight. Repair of sashes often requires removing some panes of glass, so it is best not to allow the sashes to get into such a perilous condition. Old timber can withstand decades of neglect before it loses its inherent strength, so be careful not to confuse off-putting deteriorating paint with actual timber decay.

Maintenance check-list (in order of importance)

A Moisture retention, leading to paint failure or timber decay at the ends of the frame (pulley stile, outer lining, parting bead) and corners of the timber sill.

B Severe weathering of the timber sill, leading to paint breakdown and/or timber decay.

C Failure or loosening of the lower corner joints of the sash; loss of paint and/or putty.

D Failure or loosening of sash corner joint; breakdown of putty and/or paint.

E Failure or loosening of joint between glazing bar and rail (**and/or** at the internal glazing bar joints); faults in or loss of putty and/or paint.

F Inadequate slope on the stone sill; moisture retention leading to problems with frame ends and sill.

G Inadequate or improper caulking (wrong material or poorly applied) to the junction between frame and wall.

H Build-up of paint on frame, especially parting beads, leading to stuck sashes, **or** wear on parting beads (often caused by friction from heavily painted sashes against parting beads), causing loose sashes.

I Build-up of paint on weight pocket piece.

J Damp retention in weight pocket, often exacerbated by rubbish left inside.

K Wrongly balanced weights often owing to heavier modern glass.

● All parts of the sash and frame can be taken apart for repair, and most jobs can be done *in situ*. A growing number of joiners throughout the country carry out this work and it is perfectly possible to obtain high-quality softwood from good merchants. If work is done for the first time in years, take the opportunity to change all of the sash cords, and check that the parting beads are still performing as they should; if not, have them renewed. The Society for the Protection of Ancient Buildings (SPAB) have an informative booklet, *The Repair of Wood Windows,* available from their office (London 377 1644), which details the parts of the window suitable for scarfed repairs (shown with diagrams).

- Other jobs, such as unsticking the sashes, ensuring that the weights are correctly measured and applying putty, can be done by the house-owner. Always follow safety guidelines when working with power tools and chemicals (including timber preservatives and paint-strippers).

- As long as the sashes are not clogged with paint, sanding down the flat surfaces should be sufficient prior to repainting. Never strip sashes in a caustic bath. It is impossible to wash all of the caustic out again; it destroys the glue, damages the putty and can etch old glass. When painting the sashes, do so out of the frames so that you don't accidentally paint them shut. Historically the pulley stiles (the face of the frame along which the sashes slide) were not painted but rubbed with wax to protect the timber and help the sashes slide more easily.

- Do not use heat to remove putty as concentrating heat on glass causes it to shatter. Those who would like to reuse old glass (salvaged from skips etc.) should ideally contact a glazier or stained-glass artist if they feel hesitant about cutting it themselves.

- The old pulleys may be stuck, but they are not always broken. One American recipe for taking the gunk off the pulley recommends insertion in cola! Pulleys may be rusted, or may merely require oiling. If you have to buy new pulleys, go for brass if you can, even though they cost more, as the modern plastic pulley has not been proved over hundreds of years as have the brass ones. Plastic, however convenient, has a relatively short shelf-life in most of its forms.

- A well-maintained sash window should not require any extraneous draught-proofing; however, the wear from centuries of use sometimes blunts the edges and allows more ventilation than is desired. There are several varieties of patented draught-proofing systems available, all of which have advantages and disadvantages. The house-owner is advised to look at them all and question the sales representatives before deciding which to use. Weigh up the pros and cons; all will require attention/replacement in a generation, but while they work they should make a difference to the indoor climate. Beware of sealing up your house — houses and people are organic and require surprising amounts of freely circulating air to function healthily.

In southern counties, especially Cork, bow windows are ubiquitous. No one knows why, but foreign influences could be responsible: it was written in 1749 that in Cork 'balcony windows' were built in the Spanish fashion. Maintenance here must include checking the slate of the roof and the frame head below it. The little pieces of timber on the frame catch and hold up the lower sash, indicating that there are no pulleys. The frame may be solid timber and so more resistant to decay but even so check it every few years. It makes sound financial sense to maintain curved sashes as repair is a more skilled job.

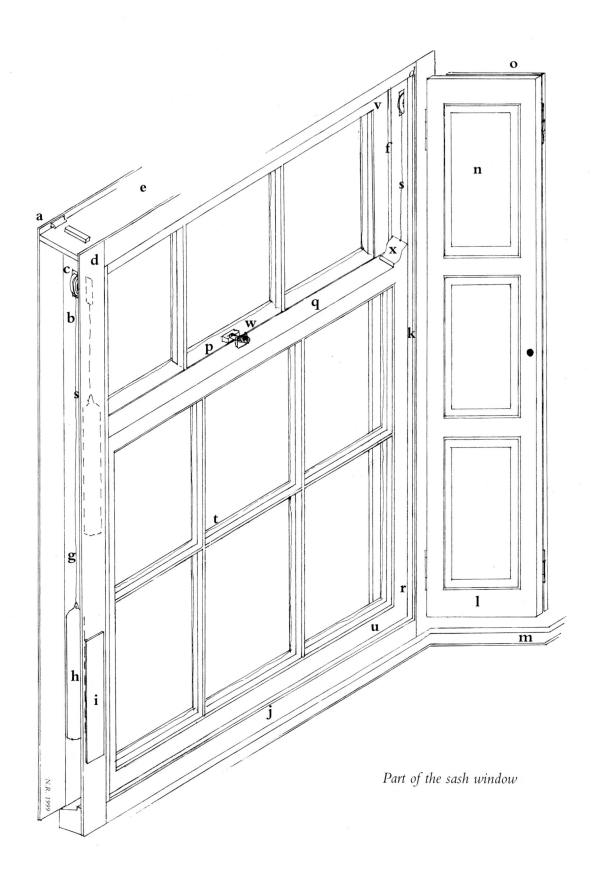

Part of the sash window

N.R. 1999

GLOSSARY

1. Parts of the window: *frame*

a   outer lining
b   pulley stile
c   pulley
d   inner lining
e   head-piece
f   parting bead
g   weight box
h   weight
i   pocket piece
j   timber sill
k   staff bead
l   shutter
m   chair rail/dado
n   shutter panel
o   shutter back-flap or leaf

2. Parts of the window: *sash*

p   top sash meeting rail
q   bottom sash meeting rail
r   sash stile
s   sash cord
t   glazing bar
u   bottom rail
v   top rail
w   meeting rail catch
x   horn

Architrave
The moulded and panelled joinery housing for a window frame on the inner face of the wall, usually containing the shutters and the timberwork bordering the inner face of the wall. A stone architrave is decorative stonework on the outside, framing the opening.

Bay window
Any window jutting out to form an interior recess. There are various types, such as bow (a curved or semicircular window) or oriel (see oriel window).

Bottom rail
See rail.

Box frame
A sash frame containing a cavity for weights.

Calme
Extruded H-sectioned lead, used to hold small quarries or squares of glass in a leaded light.

Capital
The decoratively carved head of a column.

Casement
A window that opens on hinges, almost always hinged at the sides.

Cornice
A decorative projecting moulding above a window, on the top of a building or around the ceiling of a room.

Crown glass
See p. 59.

Cylinder glass
See p. 55.

Diocletian window
A three-light window forming a semicircle, with a pier of brick or timber between each light. It is also known as a Thermal window, as the form was used extensively in the Thermae (baths) of Diocletian in Rome.

Double-hung sliding sash

A sash window with both upper and lower sashes hung by a pair of iron or lead weights, attached by cords to each sash, which run through pulleys to effectively counterbalance the weight of the sash.

Fanlight

A window placed over a door, usually with decoratively designed glazing bars of timber or compound metals. Most Irish fanlights are arched and many cover both the door and narrow windows to each side.

Fenestration

The arrangement of windows in a building.

Fixed light

Also known as a dead-light: the most basic window, which cannot open.

Frame

The case or border enclosing a pane of glass; the timber holding a light may be described as a frame, but the word more commonly means the window frame affixed into the wall. For the parts of the window frame see architrave, head-piece, inner lining, lintel, outer lining, parting bead, pulley, sill, staff bead, stile and weight.

Glazing bar

The internal grid of moulded and jointed timber lengths fixed to the stiles and rails, providing rebates for glass and structural support for the sash.

Half-sill

See sill.

Head-piece

The board across the top of the frame, into which the pulley stiles are tongued.

Horn

Also called a joggle or bracket. A small shaped projection left at the lower corners of the top sash and top corners of the bottom sash, to strengthen the corner joints. An innovation of the early nineteenth century.

Inner lining

The thin boards covering the inside of the box frame.

Latticework/latticed window
A fixed light or casement, assembled using quarries of leaded glazing, cast iron or timber in a diamond pattern.

Leaded light
Glazing consisting of small glass panes held with soldered lengths of lead in an iron or timber frame, worked in a diamond or square pattern.

Light
An aperture for admitting light, either a single glazed frame or a single opening in a wall.

Lintel
The horizontal members supporting the masonry above the head of the window.

Lunette
A window shaped like a half-moon, usually a single light.

Margin sash
A sash with a thin border of panes and a large pane (or several normal ones) in the centre. Many mid- and late nineteenth-century examples have coloured glass in the narrow panes.

Meeting rail
See rail.

Meeting rail catch
A metal fastener set with one part on the meeting rail of each sash, to bring together the sashes when closed.

Mullion
A vertical prop, of stone or timber, supporting a window frame, against which casement or sash lights close or move.

Oriel window
An overhanging projecting window, sometimes set upon corbels or cantilevered (i.e. not reaching down to the ground).

Outer lining
The thin boards covering the outside of the box frame.

Palladian window
See Venetian window.

Parting bead
A narrow piece of timber running the length of the pulley stile, fixed to the centre of the stiles and head, to hold the top and bottom sashes apart; usually fitted into a groove.

Pedestal
The foot or base of a pillar.

Pocket piece
The small rectangular board fitted into the inner lining or pulley stile, which can be removed for access to the weights.

Pulley
Wheel of timber, brass or cast iron, with a housing (box or case) of timber or cast iron, placed near the top of the stile to enable the sash cord to slide through from sash to weight.

Pulley stile
See stile.

Quarry
A diamond-shaped pane of glass, the oldest shape of pane. Quarry glazing or quarry windows are those with diamond-patterned panes, also called lattice-work.

Rail
A horizontal timber member in sash or frame. The upper sash has a top and meeting rail, the lower one has a meeting and bottom rail. In joinery work (including shutters) vertical framing boards are called stiles, while the horizontal ones are called rails.

Sash
A frame holding either one or several panes of glass, made up of vertical stiles on each side, horizontal top rail, meeting rail and bottom rail, and glazing bars (at most periods).

Sash cord
Fine cotton, hemp or jute rope attached to the sashes and weights.

Sash window
The term applied to a window with two vertically sliding lights which are opened and closed by a counterbalanced weight and pulley mechanism.

Serlian window
See Venetian window.

Shaft
The part of a column between the base and the capital.

Shutters
Panelled timber boards, corresponding to the dimensions of the opening, in pairs with one or more leaves, side-hung and hinged to fold back into the internal reveal of the window. Shutters are usually fitted into a purpose-built box.

Sill
The thick timber plank at the base of the window frame on which the lower sash sits. In Ireland timber sills are narrow, and do not project out further than the bottom sash, called the half-sill. In Britain the sill is the full width of the frame. The stone or brick window-sill is the projecting piece of masonry which helps throw water off the bottom of the window and away from the timber-work.

Single-hung sliding sash
A sash window in which one sash, usually the lower one, is counterbalanced.

Staff bead
Lengths of beading tacked onto the sides of the frame beside the lower sash, stiles and rails to keep it in place whether closed or open.

Stile
The vertical timber members of a window sash and the sides of the frame. The main upright is termed the pulley stile when in a cased frame fitted with pulleys for counterbalanced weights.

Stone sill
A projecting block of stone under the window frame, usually slightly bevelled.

Timber sill
See sill.

Top rail
See rail.

Transom
A horizontal staff of timber or stone, supported by a mullion, which usually facilitates a taller opening.

Tripartite window
A generic name for a three-light window, often a flat-arched adaptation of the Venetian arrangement. A late eighteenth-century type with timber mullions is termed the 'Wyatt window' after one of its proponents, the English architect James Wyatt. A leaded window with two mullions (of timber or stone) could also be termed a tripartite window.

Venetian window
A three-light window with a round-arched central light flanked by narrow sidelights. The narrow dividing piers are of masonry. The window may be decorated in the Doric, Ionic or Corinthian order, and given a balustraded apron.

Weight
A thin, oblong or cylindrical object of lead or cast iron, attached by a sash cord to each side of a sash, to counterbalance and enable levered opening. Weights are housed on the inside of the pulley stile, in a weight box, and are accessed by a cavity in the stile wall which is usually blocked by a length of timber called a pocket piece.

Weight box
The cavity in the frame to accommodate the weights.

Wyatt window
A late eighteenth-century three-light window with timber mullions, named after the English architect James Wyatt.

In Kinsale the ever-decreasing numbers of sash windows are generally treated well, as here, where these small but perfectly proportioned windows contribute positively to the streetscape. If there were no people in the picture it would be difficult to gauge the size of the windows. Note that the narrow window to the left has been inserted later but with an eye to fitting it into the overall pattern.

FURTHER READING

The text of this book is based on research carried out for a Ph.D. in architecture at Heriot-Watt University, Edinburgh. There are no published works devoted to the development of windows in Ireland, but the following list may be helpful as the books are interesting in their own right and the authors do discuss some aspects of fenestration. The section on conservation contains some publications that must be sent away for, which is inconvenient but unavoidable. Others may be available in your local or regional library.

Architecture

Anon. 1883 Specimens of eighteenth-century house joinery. *Irish Builder* **xxv** (15 February), 52–4.

Building of Bath Museum and Bath City Council 1994 *Windows*. Bath. Building of Bath Museum.

Calloway, S. 1994 *The elements of style*. London. Mitchell Beazley.

Casey, C. and Rowan, A. 1993 *North Leinster: the counties of Longford, Louth, Meath and Westmeath*. The Buildings of Ireland, vol. 2. Harmondsworth. Penguin.

Clifton-Taylor, A. 1987 *The pattern of English building*. London. Faber.

Craig, M. 1952 *Dublin 1660–1860*. London. [Revised by the author, 1992. London. Penguin.]

Craig, M. 1977 *Classic Irish houses of the middle size*. London. Architectural Press.

Craig, M. 1982 *The architecture of Ireland from the earliest times to 1880*. London. Batsford.

Cruickshank, D. 1985 *A guide to the Georgian buildings of Britain and Ireland*. London. Weidenfeld and Nicholson.

Cruickshank, D. and Burton, N. 1990 *Life in the Georgian city*. London. Viking.

Danaher, K. 1975 *Ireland's traditional houses*. Cork. Mercier Press.

de Breffny, B. and ffolliott, R. 1975 *The houses of Ireland*. London. Thames and Hudson.

Drury, P. 1991 Timber construction—joinery. *Architect's Journal* (14 August), 36–41.

Geoghegan, J. 1945 Notes on Dublin houses. *Dublin Historical Record* **vii** (2), 41–54.

Georgian Society 1909–13 *Georgian Society records of eighteenth-century architecture and decoration in Dublin* (5 vols). Dublin. [Reprinted by Irish University Press, 1969.]

Gray, A.S., Sambrook, J. and Halliday, C. 1990 *Fanlights, a visual architectural history*. London. Alphabooks.

Guinness, D. and O'Brien, J. 1992 *Great Irish houses and castles*. London. Weidenfeld and Nicholson.

Guinness, D. and Ryan, W. 1971 *Irish houses and castles*. London. Weidenfeld and Nicholson.

Irish Georgian Society Bulletin 1958–98 [38 vols—includes many articles on Irish architecture.]

Louw, H.J. 1983 The origin of the sash-window. *Architectural History* **26**, 49–72.

Louw, H.J. 1987 The rise of the metal window during the early industrial period in Britain. *Construction History* **3**, 31–54.

Louw, H.J. 1991 Window-glass making in Britain *c.* 1660–*c.* 1860, and its architectural impact. *Construction History* **7**, 47–66.

Louw, H.J. and Crayford, R. 1998 A constructional history of the sash-window *c.* 1670–*c.* 1725. Part 1. *Architectural History* **41**, 82–130.

Louw, H.J. and Crayford, R. 1999 A constructional history of the sash-window *c.* 1670–*c.* 1725. Part 2. *Architectural History* **42**, 173–239.

MacDonald, F., MacConville, H. and Doyle, P. 1997 *Ireland's earthen houses*. Dublin. A. & A. Farmar.

O'Brien, J. with Guinness, D. 1994 *Dublin, a grand tour*. London. Weidenfeld and Nicholson.

O'Dwyer, F. 1995 Proportion and the Georgian window. In T.J. Fenlon (ed.), *The town—conservation in the urban area: conference proceedings*, 29–35. Dublin. Irish Georgian Society.

Pfeiffer, W. and Shaffrey, M. 1990 *Irish cottages*. London. Weidenfeld and Nicholson.

Roche, N. 1996–7 The glazing fraternity in Ireland in the seventeenth and eighteenth centuries. *Irish Georgian Society Bulletin* **38**, 66–94.

Roche, N. 1998 Capturing the light: window-glasshouses in Georgian Ireland. *Irish Architectural and Decorative Studies* **1**, 194–9.

Rothery, S. 1997 *A field guide to the buildings of Ireland*. Dublin. Lilliput Press.

Rowan, A. 1979 *North-west Ulster: the counties of Londonderry, Donegal, Fermanagh and Tyrone*. The Buildings of Ireland, vol. 1. Harmondsworth. Penguin.

Sadleir, T.U. and Dickinson, P.L. 1915 *Georgian mansions in Ireland*. Dublin.

Sambrook, J. 1989 *Fanlights*. London. Chatto and Windus.

Shaffrey, P. 1975 *The Irish town, an approach to survival*. Dublin. The O'Brien Press.

Shaffrey, P. and Shaffrey, M. 1983 *Buildings of Irish towns*. Dublin. The O'Brien Press.

Shaffrey, P. and Shaffrey, M. 1985 *Buildings of the Irish countryside*. Dublin. The O'Brien Press.

Somerville Large, P. 1995 *The Irish country house*. London. Sinclair Stevenson.

Somerville Large, P. 1996 *Dublin, the fair city*. London. Sinclair Stevenson.

Williams, J. 1994 *A companion guide to architecture in Ireland, 1837–1921*. Dublin. Irish Academic Press.

Conservation

Brereton, C. 1991 *The repair of historic buildings—advice on principles and methods*. London. English Heritage.

Barrell, T. 1993 An open and shut case—keeping sash-windows in working order. *Period Living and Traditional Homes* (September), 92–4.

Davey, A., Heath, B., Hodges, D., Ketchin, M. and Milne, R. 1978 *The care and conservation of Georgian houses*. London. Architectural Press.

Department of the Environment 1996 *Conservation guidelines*. Dublin.

English Heritage 1991 *Framing opinions*. Series of eight advisory leaflets on window and door conservation. London.

Environment Service 1994 *An owner's guide—listed historic buildings of Northern Ireland*. Belfast.

Feilden, B. 1982 *The conservation of historic buildings*. London. Butterworths.

Georgian Group (n.d.) *Windows*. Georgian Group Guides, no. 1. London.

Historic Scotland 1994 *Performance standards for timber sash and case windows*. Technical Advice Note 3. Edinburgh.

Leeke, J. 1991 Sash window workshop. *Old House Journal* (September–October), 31–5.

Leeke, J. 1995 A window on sash repair. *Old House Journal* (May–June), 46–51.

Myers, J.H. 1981 *The repair of historic wooden windows*. Preservation Briefs: 9. Washington D.C. National Park Service, Preservation Assistance Division.

New York Landmarks Conservancy 1992 *Repairing old and historic windows*. Washington. The Preservation Press.

O'Donnell, B. 1986 Troubleshooting old windows. *Old House Journal*

(January–February), 16–23.

Oram, R., Pierce, R. and Coey, A. 1984 *Taken for granted*. Belfast. Environment Service.

Royal Institute of Architects in Ireland 1995 *Conservation guidelines*. Dublin.

Thornton, M. 1988 Renovation—understanding sash windows. *Period Home* (July), 85–6.

Thornton, M. 1991 Virtue and ventilation. *Traditional Homes* (May), 86–90.

Thornton, M. 1991 The well-fitted window. *Period Living and Traditional Homes* (June), 94–6.

Townsend, A. and Clarke, M. (n.d.) *The repair of wood windows*. SPAB Technical Pamphlet 13. London.